# deliverance from DAILY GIANTS

## THE POWER TO CONQUER WORRY, FEAR, FAILURE, AND OTHER GOLIATHS

### DWIGHT M. GUNTER II

BEACON HILL PRESS

OF KANSAS CITY

**Library of Congress Cataloging-in-Publication Data**

Gunter, Dwight M., 1960-
    Deliverance from daily giants : the power to conquer worry, fear, failure, and other
goliaths / Dwight M. Gunter II.
        p. cm.
    Includes bibliographical references (p.  ).
    ISBN-13: 978-0-8341-2279-6 (pbk.)
    ISBN-10: 0-8341-2279-0 (pbk.)
  1. Spiritual warfare. I. Title.

    BV4509.5.G84  2006
    248.8'6—dc22

                                                        2006029545

10  9  8  7  6  5  4  3  2  1

To Karan, a means of God's grace to me

# CONTENTS

# FOREWORD

If you enjoy reading, as I do, how many times have you located a catchy titled book in your favorite bookstore, only to discover it has no relevance for you. The attractive book with the promising title was only a mirage.

Dwight M. Gunter's *Deliverance from Daily Giants: The Power to Conquer Worry, Fear, Failure, and Other Goliaths* is not such a book. It has significant relevance, for anyone, whether or not he or she is "religious." Read a few pages; you will find it speaking to you.

If you are struggling with change and have failed, here's a book for you. It was designed to give you true, solid hope that comes through the transforming power of your Creator, who knows and loves you—just as you are!

This is no self-help book. You have already discovered that your self is impotent in effecting needed changes. Apart from God, you have no resources for personal transformation. That's not bad news but good news; for Christ came to save failures—like Dwight Gunter and the person recommending this book. Those who are "more than conquerors" (Rom. 8:37) are not people who go about patting themselves on the back! When such people see others whose lives are disordered and wrecked, they whisper, "There go I—but for the grace of God!"

This small, well-written, power-packed volume was written by one who always signs himself simply, "In the grip of grace." It's all about God's marvelous grace. Its stories are from people sharing with us how Christ has changed their existence. It's about those who now find themselves "more than conquerors" through Christ Jesus the Lord. Read these pages, yielding and trusting Christ to transform your life.

—William M. Greathouse
Former President, Trevecca Nazarene University

# MORE THAN CONQUERORS

**POWER** is a valuable commodity, and it always has been. Throughout history, nations have gone to war and lives have been lost in the quest for power. Volumes have been written about how to get power, keep power, use power—even how to abuse power. When we think we have power, we stand a little straighter and hold our heads a little higher. We know when we have it. And we know when we don't.

We even saturate our speech with power language. We talk about red as a power color. People attend power lunches. Workers sometimes take power naps. Athletes quench their thirst with Power-Ade. Power is plainly on our minds. You might even say our society is obsessed with it!

To not have power can be distressing. We find this in our language too. Blue is not a power color. In fact, *blue* is often used to describe depression and sadness. Ever had the blues? Ever felt like singing the blues? If red is the color of the powerful, could blue be the color of the powerless?

With all this emphasis on power, a person may wonder whether power is good or bad. Many times it seems to be bad. But what we have to remember is that the quality of power depends upon what it is conquering. If it is used to overcome something negative or evil, power can be good—even necessary.

Let me share with you a couple of stories from people who have been powerless in life but who have found the source of a special kind of power—a power that changed their lives. Here is Teresa's story:

When I was growing up, I was forced to go to church with my aunt and my three sisters. We went every time the door was open. The preacher would talk about hellfire and brimstone, and I was baptized out of fear of God and hell. I swore to myself that when I grew up, I would have no part of a punishing, "get you" God.

I became rebellious toward religion and God. I discovered alcohol and drugs, and they were my god for a very long time. I was again baptized, but this time in the hope it would help me stop some behaviors that were hurting others and myself—but I repeated the behaviors and blamed the god of my childhood.

At age 42 I was homeless and living in Florida. Nashville was my hometown and I returned home . . . in more ways than one. I'm working on 11 years clean and sober, and I have now found the God who is not a "get you" God but One who loves me unconditionally and One who has always been there for me, even in my addiction.

The last two years have been full of anxious moments—I faced three brain aneurisms and two brain surgeries. I then had an allergic reaction to the stint in my brain, and the doctor did not think I would make it through the night, but God was there and now I am here. I was saved by God's grace and by that same grace I am committed to grow in my relationship with my Savior. There is a power available to defeat the giants of my life . . . it is the power of God.

David found that same life-changing power:

From an early age, I remember my mother singing to me "Jesus Loves Me." Growing up in church gave me the opportunity to accept Jesus as my Savior in my teen years. But as most young adults, I couldn't wait to get out from under my parents' roof. I hated my father for what I felt was an abusive relationship, so I stayed away from home as much as possible.

The Lord was good to me. He kept me from harm, opened doors, and provided for me. But before long I gave in to temptation. Alcohol abuse led to drug abuse and then to immoral sex. I even got to the place several times where I just didn't care to live anymore and attempted to take my own life. I had forgotten the words my mother sang to me.

I walked away from God for over 20 years, crying out to Him only when I couldn't find a way to help myself anymore. In 2000, I moved to Nashville. Looking back, I now realize it was the Lord who led me here, out of a life I couldn't escape on my own. And still, I rejected Him.

**YES, JESUS LOVES ME!**

For two years a friend witnessed to me fervently, yet gently. But after a while he gave up on me, thinking I would never change. All that time, I wanted to belong, to find the answers, but I didn't really know the Way.

In 2002 my mother was diagnosed with cancer and started chemotherapy treatments. It broke my heart to watch her go through the hardest trial of her life—and the hardest trial of mine. One day she said to me, "I'm ready to meet Jesus, and I want to welcome you there someday, my son."

I asked my friend for prayer and he invited me to his church's sunrise service on Easter Sunday morning. It was my first visit to Trevecca Community Church. The Holy Spirit was so real and so present that I cried most of that day, renewing my relationship with Jesus Christ. How could I have let more than 20 years slip away? How could I have been so cruel to the people who loved me?

The Lord started changing my life that day. He took away those issues that had held me in captivity for such a long time. He put His Spirit in me and gave me the power to live in right relationship with Him.

Today my mother is cancer-free, and the miracle of His grace and power in my life has changed me forever. I want to love Him more, belong to His family, become like Him, serve Him, and introduce others to Him—just as my friend did for me.

"Yes, Jesus loves me!"

Teresa and David discovered a radical, life-changing truth: God gives us the power to conquer the enemies, the mountains, the obstacles, the baggage, the issues—whatever label you choose—in our lives. Paul makes this totally clear in Rom. 8:37: "In all these things we are more than conquerors through him who loved us."

Our world is filled with irony. People are exercising and seeking physical strength in record numbers, yet our world is plagued with weakness of character. We have more sophisticated security devices than any other time in history, yet we live in constant fear. Our civilization continually emphasizes the acceptance of almost everyone, yet many people live in isolation. Our society spotlights winners and success stories so vividly that we slink into the shadows when we experience failure. Is there any way to make sense out of the rampant confusion?

Our world is also filled with anger. Watch the news. Read the paper. People are angry. Angry at an absentee dad. Angry at an abusive mom. Angry at an unfaithful spouse. Angry with a rebellious child. Angry with the government. Even angry with God. In fact, road rage has now been renamed as intermittent explosive disorder (IED) in an attempt to blame it on something other than out-of-control anger. The prevalence of anger can make you wonder if there is any way to get past it and lead an emotionally and relationally healthy life.

And our world is filled with tragedy. What family—what individual—has not been impacted by tragedy? The loss of a child, a parent, a brother or sister? The heartbreak of 9/11 reminded us (as if we needed reminding) that tragedy is a part of our world. It's a part of life, and we can't just change the channel. Yet tragedy leads us to an even deeper issue—the struggle with evil in our world. How do we come to terms with the overwhelming pain of life?

All of these issues eventually make us hunger for the answers. We need to know if there is a way to deal with life. Is there hope for us as long as we are living in this world? Teresa and David believe there is!

This book is about the power to conquer. But don't assume that this is a self-help book. Far from it! Although you may grapple with anger and tragedy and other enemies to your soul, you'll discover that conquering is not about your ability. Rather, it's all about God's ability.

Let's consider the words of Paul again.

- *"In all these things . . ."* Every issue, every problem, every enemy, every challenge—get the idea?
- *". . . we are more than conquerors . . ."* The Greek form used here means *it is a fact* (without a doubt) *that we are* (in the present tense) *continually more than* (far beyond) *victorious!*

- "*. . . through him . . .*" It is not in our own strength, nor by our own power, but by the power of the Lord. It is *only* through Jesus Christ that we can be more than victorious.

- "*. . . who loved us.*" Paul concludes with the motivation. David's mom was right: "Jesus loves me, this I know." Jesus took the initiative to set us free. It was His idea, not ours. It was His vision first. He saw you free—whole—*victorious.* Jesus alone can make it a reality. Only He can give you the power to conquer. And He'll do it in you—because He loves you!

Are there obstacles or problems in your life that you're tired of trying to conquer on your own? Are you frustrated by your failed attempts at self-improvement? Is your energy drained of all desire to try again because you expect the same disastrous results as before?

Look deep into your heart. Better yet, allow the Holy Spirit to look into your heart with you. Do you find there the slightest desire to change? If so, read on. The source of spiritual strength is available to everyone, yet it remains untapped by most. Just open up to it, and you, too, will find the power to conquer the obstacles in your life.

# POWER TO CONQUER FEAR

**WHAT** frightens you? Do you have any fears
in your life? If someone has an overwhelming, stifling fear, we often refer to
it as a *phobia*. A phobia can be defined as
an intense and persistent fear of a specific object, situation, or activity. Because of
this intense and persistent fear, the pho-
bic person often leads a constricted life.
The anxiety is typically out of proportion
to the real situation, and the victim is fully aware that the fear is irrational. Five
million Americans have a phobia of some
sort.

You've probably heard of claustro-
phobia, which is the fear of closed or
tight spaces. You may be familiar with
acrophobia, the fear of heights. In fact,
I've battled that myself a time or two. But
have you heard of soceraphobia? That's

the fear of parents-in-law. I didn't make that up. That's an actual working term.

## THERE'S A SNAKE IN THE POOL!

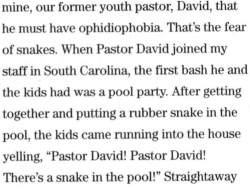

I like to joke with a good friend of mine, our former youth pastor, David, that he must have ophidiophobia. That's the fear of snakes. When Pastor David joined my staff in South Carolina, the first bash he and the kids had was a pool party. After getting together and putting a rubber snake in the pool, the kids came running into the house yelling, "Pastor David! Pastor David! There's a snake in the pool!" Straightaway he ran out to the pool with a take-charge bravado. The water feeding into the pool had a little current moving, so the rubber snake was wiggling very similar to a real one. David saw the snake and he was studying the situation from the side of the pool when suddenly someone pushed him in. He didn't even get wet! It was the most hilarious thing I've ever seen in my life! How can you fall into a pool full of water and not even get wet? I am not kidding you—he didn't! He was in and out of that water faster than the water could grab hold of his clothes. Well, maybe he was a little damp.

There are phobias from A to Z—everything from allodoxaphobia, which is the fear of opinions, to zelophobia, the fear of jealousy. After learning about some of these phobias, I made a top 10 list of my favorite ones. I think half the world suffers from Nos. 10 and 9 on my list—phronemophobia, which is the fear of thinking, and neophobia, which is the fear of anything new. A lot of people also have No. 8, ecclesiophobia, the fear of church. If you suffered from a combination of Nos. 7 and 6, kathisophobia, the fear of sitting down, and homilophobia, the fear of sermons, you'd never come to church. I don't have No. 5, geniophobia, which is the fear of chins, except when they start to stack up on me. Some people I know have No. 4, trichophobia, or the fear of hair. I also think I've met a few folks with No. 3, ablutophobia, which is the fear of washing or bathing. No. 2 can paralyze leaders—it's decidophobia, or the fear of making decisions. Finally my all-time favorite phobia, No. 1 on my list— I had to check my spelling twice on this one—is hippopotomonstrosesquippedaliophobia. I promise you, I'm not making this up—hippopotomonstrosesquippedaliophobia. And the sad thing is, if you have that phobia, you can't tell anybody, because it's the fear of long words. It seems to me that the doctor who identified that fear should have said, "We're going to call it 'H.P.' for short." You shouldn't give the poor sufferers of this fear such a long word for it because then they're going to fall to pieces just trying to tell you what they have.

So 5 million Americans have a phobia of some sort, and the rest are probably just afraid to admit it—being phobophobics, no doubt. Those people could say with Franklin Roosevelt, "The only thing we have to fear is fear itself."

Fear has plagued us since the dawn of humanity. As a matter of fact, we find the first mention of fear in Scripture in Gen. 3. Right after Adam and Eve sinned against God, they heard Him coming down to meet with them. They suddenly realized they were naked, so they went and hid themselves.

God was calling out to them, "Where are you?" Adam spoke up and God asked, "Why are you hiding?" Adam answered Him by saying, "I heard you in the garden, and I was afraid because I was naked, so I hid" (v. 10). Maybe Adam had gymnophobia, the fear of being naked.

There seems to be a connection between sin entering the world and the fear in our lives. That's not to say that having phobias or fears of any sort means we have blatant, unconfessed sin in our lives or we're not in a right relationship with God. But if you trace the topic of fear throughout Scripture, you'll find it entering the world after sin. The last mention of fear in the Bible is in Rev. 21, when John is recounting his vision of the New Jerusalem descending from heaven. John says that at no time will the gates of this holy city ever be shut (v. 25). A city's gates were usually closed at night to keep enemies out. An enemy was whoever the city dwellers were scared of and on their guard against. But in John's vision there are no more closed gates because there is no enemy, no cause or reason for fear. So it seems that the exit of fear is connected to the exit of sin in the world. But we live between fear's entrance into and its exit from the world, so we must deal with it.

So what frightens you? God understand that we have fears. There are over 1,500 verses in the Bible about fear. People who research this sort of thing say there are 365 verses that say, "Do not be afraid" or "Fear not." In a short section of only 6 verses in Matt. 10, Jesus tells us three times, "Do not be afraid."

Before He says this, Matthew records, in chapter 9, that Jesus has been going around all of the towns and villages, preaching the good news and teaching in synagogues, healing people and doing great things (v. 35). In verses 37 and 38 He told His disciples, as they looked at the crowds, "The harvest is plentiful." In other words, there are people everywhere who are lost, lonely, plagued by fear, hurting, trapped in sin—there are people everywhere in deep spiritual need. Pray that the Lord of the harvest will send workers into His field.

Then in chapter 10, beginning in verse 1, He sends the disciples out into the fields of harvest to do what He has been doing. Everything He has done leads up to this mission. First, He modeled it. Then He said, "Let's pray about it." And finally, now, He sends the workers, the disciples, out into the fields to preach, to teach, to heal, to see the people as sheep without a shepherd, and to bring good news to them.

Jesus understands that during this mission His disciples will have moments of fear. There will be times when fear will grip their souls. We're not talking here about the fear of snakes. If you have a fear of snakes, you just don't get around them. If you have a fear of heights, you just don't go up there. If you have a fear of spiders, you carry around a big shoe or something like it. We're not talking about those kinds of fears. We're talking about the deeper fears, those worries in your life that sometimes wake you up in the middle of the night and cause you to break out in a sweat wondering what will happen if this thing or that event occurs. We all have those sorts of fears.

Jesus understands that we will have to deal with fear—that we will face it as we live out life the way He wants us to live and as we tell people the Good News. He knows there will be obstacles that will creep into our lives and frighten us.

So what do we do about fear? Jesus begins to tell us how to conquer fear, and the first thing He says to us is, "Revere Me." Look at Matt. 10:26-31:

> So do not be afraid of them. There is nothing concealed that will not be disclosed, or hidden that will not be made known. What I tell you in the dark, speak in the daylight; what is whispered in your ear, proclaim from the roofs. Do not be afraid of those who kill the body but cannot kill the soul. Rather, be afraid of the One who can destroy both soul and body in hell. Are not two sparrows sold for a penny? Yet not one of them will fall to the ground apart from the will of your Father. And even the very hairs of your head are all numbered. So don't be afraid; you are worth more than many sparrows.

Let's look closer at what Jesus says in verse 28. He uses the word *afraid* or *fear,* depending on which translation you read. The word as it's used here means "to be in awe of, to have a respect for, or to revere." So what He's saying here is, don't be afraid of the ones who can kill the body and only the body; be afraid of the one who can destroy both body and soul in hell. The first time He uses the word *afraid,* it means don't start doing something that you aren't doing yet. The second time, it's a command for a simple action in the future.

Let me explain what I mean by this and why this is im-

portant. When Jesus delivered these words to His disciples,
they didn't have anything to avoid being afraid of yet. They
were in Jesus' presence; life was good while He was with
them. They were with the One who was raising the dead, giving sight to the blind, healing every
manner of disease, and speaking up to
the religious authorities of the day. He
was virtually untouchable—or so the
disciples thought. They were with Him,
so they didn't have any fear.

# WHAT IF THIS HAPPENS?

But by the time Matthew recorded
Jesus' words to His disciples, things had
changed, just as Jesus said they would.
Times of fear did indeed creep into their lives, even as they do
into ours—times that seize our souls, grip our hearts, and cause
us to think, *I'm afraid of what might happen. I'm afraid of
this situation. I'm afraid of this disease. What if this happens
to my children? What if that happens to my spouse? What if I
lose my job? What if . . .* To His disciples and to us Jesus is saying: "Don't go there. Get your perspective straight."

So in these two verses, Jesus is addressing our perspective. Are you going to live in fear of someone or something
that can kill you? Actually, I'll admit that's a pretty healthy
fear. But what about the One who has more power than someone who can only kill the body? Jesus is saying, "Let's get the
right perspective: God is greater than anything else that could
cause us to fear." We need to remember that, because when
fear begins to grip us, we start to lose perspective.

Remember the definition of *phobia* that I gave at the beginning of this chapter—an irrational and persistent fear? When this fear takes over, you start to lose perspective. So God says, "Now wait a minute. Stop. Respect Me. Revere Me. Understand first My identity, who I am, and understand My power, that I am greater than anything else you might fear." And then the fear will begin to subside. We can live, instead, in this healthy fear—this respect—of God.

There are two extremes to avoid. One extreme says, "Oh no, God's going to get me. I can't do anything. If I breathe wrong, or if I say anything wrong, then God's going to wipe me out." That's not who our God is. God's not out to get us; He's out to save us.

The other extreme is to say, "I can do anything I want to do because God's not going to bother me. God won't harm me." This extreme does not take into account the consequences of our choices as given to us in God's Word. This view does not believe God will hold us accountable. It is a very dangerous perspective.

Yet somewhere in the balance there is a *healthy* fear of God that says, "I know who God is and I know His power and I'm going to live in awe of His authority, His control. I'm going to revere Him." That helps us gain the proper perspective and conquer our fear.

But Jesus not only says, "Revere Me" but also says, *"Acknowledge Me."* In Matt. 10:32-33, Jesus says, "Whoever acknowledges me before men, I will also acknowledge him before my Father in heaven. But whoever disowns me before men, I will disown him before my Father in heaven." So Jesus is saying, "Acknowledge Me." *Acknowledge* means "to confess"—to confess Him, to give Him praise, to acknowledge who He is. *Disown* means "to deny"—to reject Him, to refuse Him.

What Jesus is pointing out is, "As you live the Christian life, fulfill the will of God, and go about the business of doing what I've called you to do and what I want you to do, you're going to have fear. You need to respect Me, but you also need to acknowledge Me. Confess Me. Acknowledge that I am the Source of your strength. Realize that you are totally dependent on Me." Much of the time, as our fear begins to surface, we think, *Hold on just a minute, Lord. I'm afraid of this situation. I'm afraid of what might happen.* And we look at our situation as if the whole picture depends upon our own strength, our own ability, our own knowledge, and our own wisdom. But that's not the case. We need to remember, when we face those situations, God is in charge. God is in control. And if God is in control and I acknowledge that fact and confess that truth, then I begin to put the fear in the right perspective. I begin to realize that it's not up to me to keep from failing. God will give success in the areas where He wants me to succeed if I keep Him first.

Jesus says, "Acknowledge me before men [and] I will . . . acknowledge [you] before my Father." Where is Jesus right now? He's at the right hand of the Father. What is He doing? He's praying for us. Can you picture Jesus as He looks at us? He says, "Father, I know her. She's one of Mine. She confesses Me. She acknowledges Me. She's not ashamed to be called by My name. And I know what causes her fear. And I pray, Father, that You'll give her power to conquer that fear." That's what Jesus is praying for us right now. So we acknowledge Christ and He acknowledges us before the Father. And then we acknowledge, *We can't do it, Lord. We can't overcome the stress. We can't overcome the problem, but God, we're totally dependent on You. We confess our total, complete reliance on You.*

So Jesus says, "Revere Me. Acknowledge Me." And then He says, "If you really want to conquer your fear, *love Me.*" In Matt. 10:37, Jesus says something rather strange, something that has confused people for years: "Anyone who loves his father or mother more than me is not worthy of me; anyone who loves his son or daughter more than me is not worthy of me." So Jesus is giving us the right perspective again. He says, "Love Me."

Let's put this in the correct context. Jesus was talking to the Hebrews at that moment. He understood that in the Hebrew mind-set the family was everything. It was considered the means to eternal life. For them eternal life meant the continuation of the family from one generation to the next, so that as long as their children, their children's children, and the children after them and beyond lived, they had life, even hopefully eternal life. So family was of utmost importance. Even the greatest scripture in a Hebrew's life—the Shema (Deut. 6:4-5)—was tied to the family. After the familiar words, "Hear, O Israel: The LORD our God, the LORD is one. Love the LORD your God with all your heart and with all your soul and with all your strength," comes the admonition that every good Hebrew should internalize this and thoroughly teach it to his or her children (see vv. 6-9, 20-24).

Now alongside this lofty idea of the family, Jesus says, "Anyone who loves his father or mother . . . son or daughter" —I imagine He would have included brother, sister, husband, or wife—"more than me is not worthy of me." What a chord this must've struck. So what was He telling them—and what is He telling us? Not to love our family? Of course not! He's putting our relationships into the right perspective, because anything we love more than Christ creates an open door for fear in our lives.

Think about it: What is the greatest fear a parent faces? Losing a child! If you're a parent, you know what I'm talking about. Sometimes my kids wonder why I get strict and want to know where they are or when they'll get home at night. That sounds old-fashioned to them, but it's because I worry about them. There is a fear that troubles me at times. Whenever I am tempted to fear for my children—which can be quite often—I have to say, *Wait a minute. God, they belong to You. I trust You with them because I love You more than I love them.* Does that mean I don't love my kids? Nothing could be further from the truth. It means I have a *greater* love for them than I could ever have on my own because God gives me a greater love. You see, it's a matter of keeping everything in perspective. Anything we love more than God begins to open that door for fear to creep in. And when fear creeps in, it begins to seize our souls.

Let me give you another illustration from Scripture. Just before Jesus was taken away from His disciples and crucified, Peter said, "Lord, I'll never deny You!"

**LORD, I'LL NEVER DENY YOU!**

Jesus said, "Peter, you'll deny Me three times before the rooster crows."

Peter said, "Oh no, not me, Lord. Everyone else will, but not me."

"Three times," Jesus said.

Before the rooster crowed the next morning, Peter denied the Lord three times. Why? Because he was afraid. He even let a little girl intimidate him into denying his Lord. Peter was afraid.

Now jump forward with me to John 21. Jesus has risen from the dead. He sits on the shore cooking breakfast for the disciples. You probably remember what happens next. Peter recognizes Him, jumps out of the boat, and swims in to shore. Peter reaches Jesus, and Jesus asks him, "Do you love Me?"

"Yes, Lord. You know I love you."

Three times Jesus asked Peter, "Do you love Me?" (See John 21:15-17.)

Now I won't go into the terms that are used, but understand this: Peter's problem was fear. He loved himself and his own life more than he loved Christ. Even though he was a brave man, this love for himself over Christ allowed fear to creep in, and the enemy had used it previously to defeat him through his triple denial.

If we love anything more than Christ, Satan will use that to defeat us.

Jesus says, "Revere Me. Acknowledge Me. Love Me." And then He says, *"Follow Me."* In Matt. 10:38, He says, "And anyone who does not take his cross and follow me is not worthy of me." *Follow* literally means "to walk on the same road with." Jesus is saying, "I have picked up My cross and if you want to go with Me, pick yours up too. Pick up your cross and walk down the same road with Me. Follow Me. It's a road of sacrifice and servanthood. It's a road of devotion and delight. It's a road of protection and divine presence."

We must walk down the same road as Christ. What I love about Christianity is that Jesus does not say, "OK, now you go and I'll see you somewhere down the road at the end of the line" or "You go and every now and then I'll check in on you and see how you're doing." That's not what Christ says. He says, "You go and I'm going to be with you every single step of the way." He says, "I'm taking up My cross and I'm going to walk the road and I want you to walk the road with Me. Come, follow Me. Walk with Me."

In Jesus' presence, there is peace. In His presence, there is no fear.

We see this truth throughout Scripture. Deut. 31:8 says, "The LORD himself goes before you and will be with you; he will never leave you nor forsake you. Do not be afraid; do not be discouraged." In 1 Chron. 28:20, when David was giving some advice to Solomon, he said, "Be strong and courageous, and do the work. Do not be afraid or discouraged, for the

LORD God, my God, is with you. He will not fail you or forsake you." Consider the words spoken through the prophet Isaiah: "So do not fear, for I am with you; do not be dismayed, for I am your God. I will strengthen you and help you; I will uphold you with my righteous right hand" (Isa. 41:10). And it says in 2 Chron. 20:17, "Do not be afraid; do not be discouraged. Go out to face [the enemy] tomorrow, and the LORD will be with you."

God is saying that we need to *revere* Him, to put things in perspective, to understand His identity and His power. We need to *acknowledge* Him: "God, I'm totally dependent on You. I can't face this problem in my life without You. I acknowledge I need You more than anything else in the world." We need to *love* Him: "Lord, I love You more than I love anything else in the world. If something in my life starts to creep up and take over my heart, Lord, point it out." And we need to *follow* Him: "I want to follow You, Jesus, because in Your presence, there is peace."

"We live in the midst of alarms; anxiety beclouds the future; we expect some new disaster with each newspaper we read." Do you know who made that statement? Sounds as if it could be made today, doesn't it? It was Abraham Lincoln. You see, with all that is happening in our world, and all that has been happening, we have a lot of reasons to be afraid—from terrorism and disease to the state of our culture. I mean, humanly, we have every reason to be afraid. And yet, in the middle of this distress, this turmoil of the unknown-yet-possible, Jesus says, "Fear not. Don't be afraid for I am with you" (see John 6:20).

There are times when I myself have had overwhelming fears. Now I don't like to admit I have fears, not many of us do. In the culture I grew up in, it wasn't good to have fear, and you sure didn't admit it if you did. But in all honesty, there have been times when I've been afraid and the fear just has me by the throat.

I've been battling a particular fear over the past year or so. God gave me victory over it shortly before writing this book, but before that I was having some major struggles with it. It really did seem to have me in a throat hold. The fear I was having such a battle with was the fear of death.

You might be thinking, *You battled the fear of death? Don't you know that there's a heaven and you don't have to worry about it?*

Sure! I know there's a heaven. I'm not worried about what happens after I die. I settled that issue a long time ago. I'm talking about a fear of dying. I'd wake up in the middle of the night after dreaming about it. I would think, *Wait a minute. Lord, what is going on here?* And it got to be a real problem for me. I mean, it started bothering me in the daytime as well as at night. And I'd pray and pray about it.

Finally, in the middle of the night, after waking up from a dream, I felt as if everything was caving in on me. I said, *Lord, please do something about this. I really need Your help. I can't conquer this on my own.* And the Holy Spirit brought a verse of scripture to my mind: "Perfect love drives out fear" (1 John 4:18). So I interpreted that the way many people do and said, *OK, Lord, then that means I don't love You perfectly because I have this fear.*

And God patiently replied, "No. That doesn't have anything to do with it. It's not *your* perfect love for Me. It's *My* perfect love for you." John went on to write in verse 19 that we love God "because he first loved us." When I realize that God loves me perfectly, completely, then I can love Him enough to trust Him with my fear. His love drives out my fear.

I just lay there in bed that night and said, *Thank You, God, for loving me so perfectly that I can revere You, acknowledge You, love You, and follow You. You love me so perfectly. Thank You for loving me so much that I can trust You.*

Now, hear it again. Don't rush past this. God loves you perfectly, totally, completely. Nothing you can do will make God love you less. And there is nothing you can do to make Him love you more. He loves you totally. When we allow that truth to saturate our hearts, minds, and souls, fear dissipates. When the light of that truth is turned on in our lives, the darkness of fear disappears. God loves us perfectly!

So I ask again, what frightens you? What is your worst fear? Perhaps it's the fear of dying. Maybe it's the fear of your marriage failing or the fear of losing your job. Whatever fear the enemy has used to grip your soul, remember to revere God, acknowledge Him, love Him, follow Him, and trust Him. You can. He himself said in the Scriptures that since a sparrow cannot fall to the ground without His notice, you, who are more important than a sparrow, can be sure that He loves you enough to take care of you and to guide you (see Matt. 10:29-31).

You can believe it—He really does love you so much that He will help restore your perspective so you will begin to understand and comprehend His power. The renewed awareness through the Holy Spirit that Christ is on your side and by your side will finally bring you the peace and assurance that you truly have nothing to fear. You, by His Spirit, can conquer fear!

BROKEN RELATIONSHIPS

# POWER TO CONQUER BROKEN RELATIONSHIPS

# 3

WHAT does it mean to reconcile or to reach reconciliation? In the dictionary the word means "to make friendly again" or "to settle a quarrel or bring into harmony."[1] Reconciliation could mean reconciling your bank statement or reconciling yourself to the realization that you'll never reconcile your bank statement. It could even mean seeking reconciliation with the banker because you're unable to reconcile your bank statement.

For me the word *reconciliation* brings several things to mind. I see a son and father who have long been at odds with each other now hold one another tightly. I see former friends who have not spoken in years restoring their relationship. I see a husband and wife weeping as they pledge to work through their differences. What do you see when you hear the word *reconciliation?*

Biblical reconciliation can mean several things. Although the meanings are very similar, there is a slightly different nuance to each. For one thing, biblical reconciliation can involve the reconciliation or restoration of a relationship. It can also refer to the settling of hostility so that people and nations who were once enemies can now be reconciled to one another. And it can signify a real change in parties or people that succeeds in bringing them all together. All of these are facets of the biblical concept of reconciliation.

Throughout history, God has desired reconciliation. As a matter of fact, Paul wrote in 2 Cor. 5:19 that "God was reconciling the world to himself in Christ, not counting men's sins against them. And he has committed to us the message of reconciliation." So God desires reconciliation.

Have you ever been in need of reconciliation with another person? Have you ever had a relationship that was strained or stressed or severed?

I believe that God can give us the power to conquer broken relationships. But in order for that to occur we have to really begin to understand what reconciliation is all about, so I'm going to start by telling you what it is not about.

The first myth: Reconciliation means pretending or acting as if the offense never occurred. Now I know that an offense can be so small that we just have to let it go, but when an offense begins to fester and bother us and cause us to think about it multiple times, we probably ought to deal with it. Denial is not synonymous with reconciliation. Acting as if an offense didn't happen can lead to big problems, but reconciliation can lead to major solutions. Bill Hybels said, "The mark of community—true biblical unity—is not the absence of conflict but the presence of a reconciling spirit. . . . Conflict that goes underground poisons the soil and hurts everyone eventually."[2] Reconciliation does not mean acting as if the offense never occurred.

The second myth: After reconciliation, everything goes back to the way it was before the offense occurred. That's probably not going to happen. I mean, it might but probably won't. The greater the offense, the deeper the hurt, the less likely things will go back to the way they were before. Circumstances may be better, but they will probably never be the same.

The third myth: Forgiveness is synonymous with reconciliation. *Forgiveness* and *reconciliation* are two totally different words, two totally different issues. Forgiveness means to release whereas reconciliation means to bring together. You and I both know that we can forgive someone and still not be reconciled to them.

The fourth myth: If I am a Christian, I will always be able to reconcile any differences I might have with other people. Not true. As Christians, we should desire reconciliation and be willing to reconcile, but it takes two to dance to the tune of reconciliation and if one is going to sit that song out, there is nothing the other can do. That's why Paul wrote in

Rom. 12:18: "If it is possible, as far as it depends on you, live at peace with everyone."

Now that we know what reconciliation is not about, just what is it and how do we reach it? Let's look at the components of reconciliation in order to better understand the process.

When there is a need for reconciliation, there are usually two parties involved—the offender and the offended. We would like to think it is easy to tell which person is the offender and which is the offended. But when a relationship starts to deteriorate, a person usually finds that he or she is the offender *and* the offended. The lines of delineation can't be drawn so clearly. We need to be honest and take note of what the Bible says to both the offender and the offended. That's right, even the offended has a role to play—and it's not easy.

Now with that in mind, let's look at the three-step process for the offender. The offender, first of all, must confess. He or she needs to admit, "Yes, I did that. Yes, I acted that way. Yes, it was wrong. I should not have said that. I should not have done that."

In addition to confession, there also must be repentance. Confession is not the same thing as repentance. Maybe you're like I am and there have been times in your life when you've confessed but haven't repented. You might find yourself saying, "Yeah, I did it, and if you mess with me, I'll do it again!" Where's the repentance? Alongside confession a person needs to add, "I'm sorry. I don't ever want to do that again. I don't ever want to say that again. I want to be different." So the first two steps are confession followed by repentance. But wait, there's more.

The third step is a willingness to make restitution. Our attitude should be, "Yes, I did it and I wish I hadn't done it. I wish I could take it back, but I can't. So what can I do to make it right?" Before you think that step three is just my opinion, listen to what Jesus said in Matt. 5:23: "Therefore, if you are offering your gift at the altar and there remember that your brother has *something against you* . . ." In other words, you're standing at the altar and you're in an act of worship when you remember your brother has something against you. Probably the Holy Spirit is pointing that out to you in that moment. So what do you do? Jesus continues, "Leave your gift there in front of the altar. First go and be reconciled to your brother" (v. 24)—there, right there, is confession and repentance. "Settle the matter quickly with your adversary who is taking you to court. Do it while you are still with him on the way, or he may hand you over to the judge, and the judge may hand you over to the officer, and you may be thrown into prison. I tell you the truth, you will not get out until you have paid the last penny" (v. 25)—and that is *restitution.* So to reach reconciliation an offender needs to do all three steps of the process, that is, confess, repent, and make restitution.

There is a process the offended has to follow as well. First of all, the offended must forgive. Forgiveness is absolutely necessary. I have to release the offender from the debt he or she owes me. You may be thinking, *It's one thing to for-*

*give somebody when he or she does something small like cuts you off while going down the interstate, but it's another thing when the hurt is so deep that you're cut to the soul. Some issues are so big I don't think I can let them go.* However, God says to let them go. And quite honestly, I wish God would say, "When the hurt gets to such and such a level, then you don't have to let it go." But God doesn't say that. In fact, Jesus says in the Sermon on the Mount, "If you forgive men

## THERE IS A POWER IN FORGETTING.

when they sin against you, your heavenly Father will also forgive you. But if you do not forgive men their sins, your Father will not forgive your sins" (Matt. 6:14-15). Again in Mark 11:25 Jesus says, "And when you stand praying, if you hold anything against anyone, forgive him, so that your Father in heaven may forgive your sins." Those are strong words, aren't they? I have to forgive in order to stay in the forgiving grace of God!

Your response at this point may be like that of so many people: "Well, I can't do that! No way! Not me! You have no idea what this person did! I can't!" Maybe you can't forgive on your own. But the Holy Spirit, whom God has sent to us, will enable us to forgive. You may be tempted to ask, "Am I to forgive and forget?" That's not what I'm talking about. There is a power in forgetting. God can cast our offenses into the sea of forgetfulness never to be remembered against us anymore, but we might never forget the offenses of others. However, forgetting and not forgiving are two different issues. We are to forgive; we are to let it go; we are to release it. We may remember for years to come, or even forever. But we must still forgive. And this is exactly why I call this a process. We may have to forgive, again and again, reaffirming the grace active in our lives.

There is another step that may be necessary to reach the goal of reconciliation, and that is confrontation with the truth in love. Here's what I'm talking about. If someone has offended you, there could be several reasons or issues involved. The person may not even know he or she has offended you. There are some people in this world whose behavior is just plain offensive. What do you do about that? You have to confront the person, because it's not one of those petty things you can simply ignore; it really irritates you. It begins to fester and you can't get it off your mind or spirit. So you should go to the person and say, "You said this, and it really offended me." You may get a reaction like, "Oh, wow. I am so sorry. I had no idea." But if you don't go, then there is potentially a break in the relationship and the person doing the offending will wonder what happened and why you're not talking to him or her anymore. How Christian is that—to just let the unknown and the unsaid fester? In this case the offended will pay a greater price than the offender; the offense will continue to be an irritation, and the offender will not even know it.

Now it could be that the offender offended you on purpose and is not about to apologize. What are you supposed to do? You should confront the offender with the truth in love. Point out the offense lovingly and set appropriate boundaries, because you may be able to help the person learn more about how he or she should live and grow in the grace and knowledge of our Lord Jesus Christ. Listen to the words of Jesus: "If your brother sins against you, go and show him his fault, just between the two of you. If he listens to you, you have won your brother over" (Matt. 18:15). In other words, don't go out and tell everyone about what a person did to you. Go and talk to the person privately so you will have a chance to restore your relationship and attain reconciliation.

So, if the offender does what he or she is supposed to do, confesses, repents, and makes restitution, and the offended does what he or she is supposed to do, forgives, and—if necessary—confronts in love, then the result is reconciliation, or the coming back together of those who were divided.

With so many divisions today in our families, between friends, among work associates, and even in churches—the need for reconciliation is plain for all to see. Reconciliation in one form or another is needed in every area of life. One of the best ways to learn more about it and how it's done is to see it depicted in action. Not surprisingly, some of the best illustrations of reconciliation are found in the Scriptures. The story of Jacob and Esau is an especially good example.

This story climaxes in Gen. 32—33 after a history of deceit, animosity, and threats of violence. We pick up the story in chapter 27. Old and believing himself to be near death, Isaac wants to give Esau his blessing. So he tells Esau to go kill an animal, cook the meat, and bring the meal to him and he will bless Esau. Rebekah, Esau's mother, however, overhears the conversation between Isaac and Esau and tells Jacob, Esau's brother, what is about to happen. Knowing that Isaac is almost blind, they contrive to trick him. They put goat hair on Jacob's arm to mimic Esau's hairy body, dress him in Esau's clothes (so he has the smell of the wild on him), and prepare meat the way Esau would. Then going before his half-blind father, Jacob pretends to be Esau and receives the blessing. Now in our culture today, we would reverse the blessing in the name of fraud. But in the culture of Isaac's day, you could not do that. Once it was said, it was done. And so, Isaac blesses Jacob thinking it is Esau.

A little while later Esau comes in. He has killed and prepared the meat, and he walks in before his father and says, "I'm here for the blessing." His father is now confused and says, "I've already blessed you." And then the truth begins to emerge. By the time we arrive at chapter 28, we find that the relationship between Esau and Jacob is totally severed and Esau is threatening to kill Jacob. So Jacob runs away to the house of Laban, Rebekah's brother.

Sometime later in chapter 29, Jacob falls in love with Rachel, Laban's daughter. He wants to marry Rachel, but Laban deceives him and Jacob marries Leah the older sister. Jacob is then able to marry Rachel after pledging to work more years for Laban. However, Laban continues to deceive Jacob through the years. In fact, during the years that Jacob worked for Laban, Laban changed their contract 10 times. But God kept blessing Jacob. And finally, growing tired of Laban's deceit, Jacob gathers his family, his children, his wives, his maidservants, his menservants, and his flocks, and he flees from Laban. Rather than confronting Laban as he should have, he runs away. In fact, Jacob sneaks away. Laban sees that Jacob is gone and pursues him. After Laban catches up to Jacob, they confront each other and settle their differences. In this scene, a little confession, repentance, and restitution occur. After parting with Laban on good terms, Jacob continues on his way—a way that will eventually take him to his brother, Esau.

The story continues in chapter 32, where we find Jacob on the journey to reconciliation.

Jacob also went on his own way and the angels of God met him. When Jacob saw them, he said, "This is the camp of God!" So he named that place Mahanaim. Jacob sent messengers ahead of him to his brother Esau in the land of Seir, the country of Edom. He instructed them: "This is what you are to say to my master Esau: 'Your servant Jacob says, I have been staying with Laban and have remained there till now. I have cattle and donkeys, sheep and goats, menservants and maidservants. Now I am sending this message to my lord, that I may find favor in your eyes.'" When the messengers returned to Jacob, they said, "We went to your brother Esau, and now he is coming to meet you, and four hundred men are with him."

Can you imagine Jacob's anxiety at this point in the story? He thinks, *I took his birthright. I took his blessing, and now he's coming with 400 men to meet me! I don't think this is going to be a friendly meeting.* This is not going to be a "how's life been treating you?" kind of reunion. So verses 7-8 say, "In great fear and distress Jacob divided the people who were with him into two groups, and flocks and herds and camels as well. He thought, 'If Esau comes and attacks one group, the group that is left may escape.'"

Notice Jacob's plan: divide the family in two. We're going to send one group this way and another group that way, and maybe whichever group not attacked can escape. Then, after Jacob makes his plan, he prays (v. 9): "O God of my father Abraham, God of my father Isaac, O LORD, who said to me, 'Go back to your country and your relatives, and I will make you prosper.'"

If you pause here for a moment and read between the lines, you'll hear Jacob say, *God, You told me to do this. I didn't do this on my own. God, I followed Your directions, and now it looks like I'm going to be killed. Lord, this was Your idea. This is what You wanted me to do.* Then in the quietness of this conversation with God, Jacob begins to reflect on God's grace:

> I am unworthy of all the kindness and faithfulness you have shown your servant. I had only my staff when I crossed this Jordan, but now I have become two groups. Save me, I pray, from the hand of my brother Esau, for I am afraid he will come and attack me, and also the mothers with their children. But you have said, "I will surely make you prosper and will make your de-

scendants like the sand of the sea, which cannot be counted" *(vv. 10-12)*.

Jacob is recalling the promises of God and the command of God.

Following his prayer,

he spent the night there, and from what he had with him he selected a gift for his brother Esau: two hundred female goats and twenty male goats, two hundred ewes and twenty rams, thirty female camels with their young, forty cows and ten bulls, and twenty female donkeys and ten male donkeys. He put them in the care of his servants, each herd by itself, and said to his servants, "Go ahead of me, and keep some space between the herds" *(vv. 13-16)*.

Jacob has divided all these groups into independent herds and he's sending them one at a time by the servants. The story continues in verses 17-21:

He instructed the one in the lead: "When my brother Esau meets you and asks, 'To whom do you belong, and where are you going, and who owns all these animals in front of you?' then you are to say, 'They belong to your servant Jacob. They are a gift sent to my lord Esau, and he is coming behind us.'" He also instructed the second, the third and all the others who followed the herds: "You are to say the same thing to Esau when you meet him. And be sure to say, 'Your servant Jacob is coming behind us.'" For he thought, "I will pacify him with these gifts I am sending on ahead; later, when I see him, perhaps he will receive me." So Jacob's gifts went on ahead of him, but he himself spent the night in the camp.

Now it's fascinating to me that Jacob is demonstrating his sincerity. He didn't have to return, but God commanded him to do so. And God had made some promises to him. So now he is on a journey of trust and obedience. He still believes Esau is angry and is seeking revenge, and he devises a plan that he hopes will soften Esau's anger just a little. Yet in the midst of all this, something else happens, as verses 22-28 recount:

> That night Jacob got up and took his two wives, his two maidservants and his eleven sons and crossed the ford of the Jabbok. After he had sent them across the stream, he sent over all his possessions. So Jacob was left alone, and a man wrestled with him till daybreak. When the man saw that he could not overpower him, he touched the socket of Jacob's hip so that his hip was wrenched as he wrestled with the man. Then the man said, "Let me go, for it is daybreak." But Jacob replied, "I will not let you go unless you bless me." The man asked him, "What is your name?" "Jacob," he answered. Then the man said, "Your name will no longer be Jacob, but Israel, because you have struggled with God and with men and have overcome."

Look at this scene for just a moment. Jacob plans to spend the night trying to psyche himself up in preparation for what's about to happen, but instead, God shows up in the form of a man and they begin to wrestle. The man cannot overcome Jacob, and Jacob cannot overcome the man. Now we know that God didn't need to wrestle with Jacob. If God wanted to kill Jacob, He could have just said the word, probably could have just thought it, and Jacob would be history. But there is a reason Jacob is wrestling with God and God is wrestling with Jacob. God is teaching Jacob a very important lesson: "Jacob, there are some issues with which you must struggle and grapple with Me about, issues that you can't just ignore."

While my children were growing up, I enjoyed wrestling with them. Although I could easily win a match, letting them try to beat me was good for them. In the strain of the moment, they grew, got stronger, and learned persistence. I think that's what God is like when He deals with us—He's like a father with a young child. He wrestles with us, and sometimes we may think, "I've got Him now." In reality, we're not overcoming God; God's just letting us wrestle, grapple, and strain to grow and become stronger.

So Jacob wrestles with God, and then he makes a fascinating statement right when he thinks he has a good hold on Him. Jacob says, "I will not let you go unless you bless me" (v. 26). You may think that sounds awfully self-centered and that he just wants another blessing. But that's not the case here. Remember, Jacob was about to go out and meet the man that he had wronged, the man who was coming with an army of 400 and who could destroy Jacob and all of his household. And Jacob's going because God instructed him to go and because it's the right thing to do. And so he says, "God, I have to know that I have Your blessing. I have to know I have Your approval. I have to know You're going to empower and strengthen me."

When you start to reconcile relationships and you initiate some of those difficult conversations, there is something very important you need to know. Maybe you're the offender and you have to go and confess, repent, and make restitution. Or maybe you're the offended and you have to confront someone. In either case, you have to know you are going in the strength and in the Spirit of the Lord. Jacob says, "I have to know that God is with me." And so he wrestles and begs for a blessing. God in turn blesses him, confirming His power and protection. But before Jacob even makes his request, God does something else—He touches Jacob's hip. So for the rest of Jacob's life he walks with a limp to remind him of the need for reconciliation and of the power of God at work in his life.

Before we leave this scene, let's listen to the rest of the conversation. Jacob says, "Please tell me your name." And God replies, "Why do you ask my name?" And then God blesses Jacob. You can almost see this as an aha moment for Jacob. Now he knows the One with whom he wrestles. It finally dawns on him. So he names the place Peniel, which means "face of God," saying "it is because I saw God face to face, and yet my life was spared" (vv. 29-30).

Chapter 33 tells the story of how Jacob is reconciled with Esau. Esau is on his way to see Jacob and is met by all of the various herds Jacob has sent. Finally, Jacob arrives and bows down seven times before Esau (see vv. 1-3). Then we see a remarkable picture of reconciliation: "But Esau ran to meet Jacob and embraced him; he threw his arms around his neck and kissed him. And they wept" (v. 4).

The story continues: "Then Esau looked up and saw the women and children. 'Who are these with you?' he asked. Jacob answered, 'They are the children God has graciously given your servant'" (v. 5). As the conversation proceeds, Jacob explains that the livestock he sent earlier was a gift to Esau. But Esau says, "I don't need all of this stuff. My God has blessed me. I have all I need." Jacob insists, "No, it's yours. I want you to take it." (See verses 8-10.) They probably went back and forth like this for a little while before Esau agreed to accept Jacob's gifts. What a change from the last time the brothers were together! Before, they were just looking out for themselves—how much each could get—but now restoring their relationship has become more important than all this stuff. The story ends with the two brothers parting company reconciled to each other. A relationship has been restored—and Jacob has been changed because of his encounters with God. Truly, a deep hunger to be reconciled is evidence of a changed life.

The Scriptures present compelling images of reconciliation, but images like those can be seen all around us. I've seen reconciliation enter the life of a 15-year-old boy who was angry with himself and the world and in a strained relationship with his father. Like Jacob, he wrestled with God in an open-air tabernacle at a campground, and God melted his heart. His parents were also in the tabernacle, and he started heading toward them to reconcile with his dad. But God had been speaking to his dad as well, and the two met in mid-aisle, embraced, and began a restored relationship that continues to improve to this day.

Likewise, I've seen a dad jump up from his porch and run with outstretched arms to embrace his prodigal son as he rounds the corner on his way home. I've also seen people in church who haven't spoken to each other in years get up from their seats, come together, and patch up their differences.

There are many more images I could share, but as you can see, reconciliation can occur. It just takes two—two people walking in obedience to Jesus. And when that happens, it is a beautiful thing. The relationship that was lost—the one we thought would never be reconciled—is restored.

God is telling us, "If you want to overcome broken relationships, then I'm going to empower you to do it." God was preparing the way for Jacob and Esau before their meeting, and He will do the same for us when we want to mend our relationships. That's the kind of business God is in—the relationship-mending business. Remember, relationships are the only things we take with us to heaven—not our money or our titles; not our positions or our prestige—only relationships. God desires His people to love one another. At times rifts occur among us. But God gives us the power to reconcile and seal those rifts. Do you have a relationship that needs repairing, a reconciliation that needs reaching? Then open yourself up to God's power and let Him help you with the repairs.

# POWER TO CONQUER THE PAST 4

**MEMORY** is a precious gift. I had a dream recently. My wife, Karan, and I were standing together in a house we built in 1985. Our daughter, Lindsay, was two years old at the time and had beautiful, long blond hair. In my dream, I saw her running down the hall toward me, her hair flying behind her, and then she jumped into my arms. I didn't want to wake up from that dream for a while. Maybe I'm just a dad missing his daughter now that she is married.

Memory is a precious gift.

Just the other day, Karan and I were riding around the countryside and I saw a house next to a large field. I looked at the house for a moment and said to Karan, "That's a house like my grandpa used to have, the old farmhouse, where we'd sit out on the porch." My mind immediately made a trip down memory lane. I would sit on the front porch with my grandpa, a farmer, and we would talk politics. He was a diehard southern Democrat, and we'd get into deep political discussions. We'd also talk about history, our other favorite subject. We would debate politics and talk about American history and family history for hours and hours. So I enjoyed my sweet trip down memory lane.

Memory is a precious gift—that is, it was intended to be.

You know what the word *memory* means. Memory is the recollection of the past. It's the collage in our minds formed by pictures of people, places, events—all of the things that have come into our lives to make us into who we now are. However, there are parts of our past that we would really rather forget. Sometimes we wish our memory would fail. We would choose to forget some of the things in our past if only we could, because memory is not always precious.

As we try to live our lives for Christ, even as we work to get through the most mundane aspects of our existence, this problem may keep popping up to block our way, trip us up, or bring us crashing down altogether. The problem is getting past our past.

If we are absolutely honest, we'll admit that there are some things in our past that we regret. We would like to yell, "Do over! Let's start again. Let's go back. Take it from the beginning."

If only we could.

People feel regret over all kinds of issues, like regret over a marriage or regret over divorce or regret over broken relationships of all kinds. We may regret mistakes we've made in raising our kids or bad career moves or missed business opportunities. And our regrets may go even deeper than that. Maybe we regret not following what we believed to be the will of God at a past time in our lives. Many choices or actions from our past can bring regret over sin and its consequences. Regret can spring from any number of causes in our past.

But in Phil. 3, Paul begins to talk about this issue of regretting the past. In fact, he's telling his story, giving his testimony. In this passage, he encourages us to forget those things that lie behind us. In verses 7-16, Paul writes:

> But whatever was to my profit I now consider loss for the sake of Christ. What is more, I consider everything a loss compared to the surpassing greatness of knowing Christ Jesus my Lord, for whose sake I have lost all things. I consider them rubbish, that I may gain Christ and be found in him, not having a righteousness of my own that comes from the law, but that which is through faith in Christ—the righteousness that comes from God and is by faith. I want to know Christ and the power of his resurrection and the fellowship of sharing in his sufferings, becoming like him in his death, and so, somehow, to attain to the resurrection from the dead.

> Not that I have already obtained all this, or have already been made perfect, but I press on to take hold of that for which Christ Jesus took hold of me. Brothers, I do not consider myself yet to have taken hold of it. But one thing I do: Forgetting what is behind and strain-

ing toward what is ahead, I press on toward the goal to win the prize for which God has called me heavenward in Christ Jesus.

All of us who are mature should take such a view of things. And if on some point you think differently, that too God will make clear to you. Only let us live up to what we have already attained.

Paul is addressing several problems in the church at Philippi. He's trying to deal with a group of people who are legalists. Paul is traveling around preaching the message of grace, the message of freedom in Christ, and these people are coming along behind him and saying, "If all of you who have accepted Christ really want to be Christian, you're going to have to jump through the hoops of the Law. You have to be circumcised." That was the big law of the day—you must follow the law of circumcision. In other words, "If you're going to be a good follower of Christ, you have to be a good follower of the Jewish Law first." Paul is saying, "No way. That is not the path to Christianity." He argues very strongly against that issue and begins to preach the truth of grace.

In so doing, he talks about how he dealt with his past and how we should deal with our past. In other words, there were people in the Philippian church who would have liked to forget their past—if only they could. Remember, this congregation did not grow up with the Hebrew laws and regulations. They grew up in a pagan, hedonistic, Gentile world, and as a result they had been into things they would choose to forget if they could. When someone came along teaching legalism, it struck a chord in their hearts because legalism says, if I do the right things and don't do the wrong things, I can deal with the shame of my past and then I can earn or deserve God's grace and acceptance and feel good about who I am.

# IS YOUR PAST A PROBLEM?

We'll get to Paul's response to this teaching in a minute. But first, let me ask you: Is your past a problem? Can you live it down? Is your past taking up too much of your present? Do you feel as though your future is being determined by your past?

For many people, the past is full of sadness and setback, sins and shame, and disappointments and defeats. We try to forget it, we try to move on, and we try to do better, but we just can't seem to get past our past. Just when we think it's safe to go back in the water, the accuser shows up. And he says, "But do you remember what you did? Do you remember what happened to you?" And suddenly we're defeated again.

So here's the question: *Is there power to conquer the past?*

It's very difficult to forget the past, isn't it? Oh, I can lose my train of thought. I can forget yesterday or what I was trying to say just a moment ago or the point to a story I'm trying to tell. But research tells us that we don't really forget anything that happens to us.

One reason it is so difficult to get past our past lies deep within the neurological wiring of our brain. Dr. Wilber Penfield, director of the Montreal Neurological Institute, said in a report to the Smithsonian Institute in Washington, D.C.: "Our brain contains a permanent record of our past that is like a single, continuous strip of moving film. . . . The film is like a library that records a person's whole life from childhood on. At anytime a person can relive those scenes from the past and feel almost exactly the same emotions they did during the original experience."[3]

In other words, we see a past experience in our mind's eye and most often it is accompanied by the same degree of emotion we felt in the original moment.

So can we get past the past? Is there enough power to really do that?

Let's return to Phil. 3. Again, Paul is talking about his past. Let's begin in verse 2: "Watch out for those dogs, those men who do evil, those mutilators of the flesh." It sounds as if Paul has a special place in his heart for these men. He has no use for them whatsoever, and he says, "It is we who are the circumcision, we who worship by the Spirit of God, wo glory in Christ Jesus, and who put no confidence in the flesh—though I myself have reasons for such confidence" (vv.3-4a). Now here's where Paul tells his story. He says, "If anyone else thinks he has reasons to put confidence in the flesh, I have more: circumcised on the eighth day, of the people of Israel, of the tribe of Benjamin, a Hebrew of Hebrews; in regard to the law, a Pharisee; as for zeal, persecuting the church; as for legalistic righteousness, faultless" (vv. 4b-6). And every good Hebrew of that day would have said, "Here, here, Paul. He is a man among men, a Hebrew among Hebrews."

But Paul was saying between the lines, "You may think my past is great, but you don't realize how bad I was. I was standing there, a Hebrew among Hebrews, zealous in persecuting the church, when they took a righteous man by the name of Stephen and stoned him . . . and I was giving my approval." Paul could've added, "I was on the road to Damascus with letters of authority, and what was I going to do? I was going to kill people." I wonder if he could hear in his mind the cries of the people being killed and tortured as he was writing this.

Paul might have been a scholar and he might have been accepted by the current culture, but he had things in his past he wanted to forget—as did the Philippians. Look at verses 7-8, where Paul says, "Whatever was to my profit I now consider loss for the sake of Christ. What is more, I consider everything a loss compared to the surpassing greatness of knowing Christ Jesus my Lord, for whose sake I have lost all things." Three times in two verses he uses the word *loss*. In the Greek language of Paul, *loss* and *lost* are actually the same word—a term for a business loss. It refers to something that can never be restored. The word *loss* refers to something that is gone forever. In Paul's day when something was lost at sea it was gone; it could never be recovered. It was swallowed up by the sea, end of story. That's the kind of word he's using.

Paul's language then gets even stronger. He says, "I consider them rubbish." Now there are two translations for the Greek word behind *rubbish*. One translation refers to table scraps that are thrown to the dogs. The other translation is manure, animal waste. Paul is using some strong language here because he's trying to give us a picture of what he thinks of his past. He says it is a loss, it's gone, and, even more than that, it's rubbish—it's of absolutely no use whatsoever.

## I WANT TO KNOW CHRIST!

Then Paul says, in verse 10, "I want to know Christ." Actually, it's more like he's saying, "I WANT TO KNOW CHRIST!" Can you hear the passion in his voice? "I want to know Christ! I don't care about knowing anything else in my life. I've given all that stuff up, all that garbage that was in my past. It's gone; it's behind me. I want to know Christ! I want to know the power of the resurrection and the fellowship of sharing in His sufferings!" In other words, "I want to go through whatever I have to go through to become like Him, because I want to know Him."

And when he says *know Him*, he's not talking about reading a book about Him; he's talking about knowing Christ personally. "I want to know *Him*—how He thinks, how He feels, and how He views the world. I want to think His thoughts and see His visions. In other words, I want to become like Him and then somehow obtain the resurrection from the dead so I can live forever with Him. You see, I really want to know Christ."

Out of that passion, Paul says, "I know what I'm going to do. If I'm going to know Christ, if I'm going to become like Him, if I'm going to live forever with Him, then I'm going to have to put the past in the past." Paul admits in verse 12, "Not that I have already obtained all this, or have already been made perfect, but I press on to take hold of that for which Christ Jesus took hold of me." Then Paul defined his commitment in verses 13-14: "I do not consider myself yet to have taken hold of it. But one thing I do: Forgetting what is behind and straining toward what is ahead, I press on toward the goal to win the prize for which God has called me heavenward in Christ Jesus."

Notice the use of four terms. The first term is *forgetting*. Put it out of your mind. That's what the word *forget* literally means—remove it from your thoughts. The second term is *straining*. "Forgetting what is behind and straining toward what is ahead." Have you ever seen runners in a track meet? They're on sprints and they're running and running for all their worth and, man, they have such great form. When they run, their heads are just perfectly still. It's as if all of the movement of their bodies and their energy is perfectly focused in all the right places. They finally approach the finish line, arrive at the tape, and they lean in toward it. Have you seen what I'm talking about, that leaning and stretching? That's what that word *straining* means. That's where it's taken from, that stretching toward that finish line; it's reaching with everything in you toward the tape at the end. In other words, Paul is saying, "I know where I'm going. I'm putting some things behind me and I'm stretching on to what's ahead." Those two terms can't really be separated because you can't stretch to what is ahead if there's something behind you that's dragging you down.

When we're out on a baseball diamond and I'm running

the bases, my son, Trae, makes it a habit to yell out to me, "Dad, cut loose the boat anchor." I keep dragging that boat anchor around behind me. I like my boat anchor, thank you very much. I have a lot invested in it.

But the runners with whom Paul is identifying are cutting loose everything behind them and they're straining toward that finish line. They have to get there because that's what they're after, that's where they're headed, and they know it. That's why they're in the shape they're in; they've turned loose of so much that was holding them back and now they can stretch ahead.

But then Paul gives us something else in these verses. He says you have to stretch on toward the goal to win the prize. What is the goal? The goal is winning the prize. Look at that word—*prize*. What is Paul referring to when he talks about the prize? We have to go back to verse 10 when Paul passionately cries out, "I want to know Christ." So what's the prize? It is knowing Christ, becoming like Him, and living forever with Him. That is the prize; that's what he's after. Paul is saying he has to turn loose of everything behind him, forget it, and put it in the past and then he can stretch on to the prize itself.

Now you may be thinking, *Well, I understand that I'm supposed to forget the past, but how? Where is the power for conquering the past?* The answer is in verse 12, where Paul says, "Not that I have already obtained all this, or have already been made perfect, but I press on to take hold of that for which Christ Jesus took hold of me." That's the fourth term—*took hold. Took hold* means apprehended, seized, possessed, grabbed. I studied this passage many times before I saw its connection to forgetting the past. You see, the reason my past does not determine my future, and the reason the past cannot prevent me from winning the prize, is because Jesus himself reached down and took hold of me. He's seized me, and I am in the grip of His grace. He took hold of me, dusted me off, and shook me loose from the bondage and all the strongholds the past had on me. The only way I can truly deal with the issues of the past is to realize that I am in the grip of grace and all that mattered before is now irrelevant because Jesus Christ has His hold on me.

Now don't be misled. It is possible to hang on to the baggage. Jesus can reach down and pick us up, but we can still say, "Wait a minute, Lord, I have to pick up this baggage. I have to pick up this guilt and this mistake and this wrong choice." But Jesus says to us, "No, leave them there. Don't worry anymore about them. The enemy of your soul meant for all those experiences to harm you and ruin you, but you don't own them anymore because I'm going to redeem them, change them, and use them for My glory and to advance My kingdom. You are going to run a better race because you're in My grip now—the grip of grace. I have apprehended you."

You see, it's not that we just say, "OK, OK, I'm going to forget. I'm going to forget." No, that's not it at all. It's a matter of praying, *Jesus, I have been seized by Your presence. My life is in Your hands now, so what I have done in the past does not matter any longer.*

Paul understood that when he said in Rom. 8:1, "Therefore, there is now no condemnation for those who are in Christ Jesus." The past is past. The great theologian Augustine (d. 430) wrote, "Trust the past to God's mercy, the present to God's love, and the future to God's providence." You can get past the past by the grace of God.

As I was writing these words, I asked myself, "Who in Scripture had to get past their past?" Then I began to think, "Who didn't?" So I wrote a list of those who did. It is not all-inclusive, but the point is plain to see.

- Jacob had been a thief, but he fathered a nation known as the people of God.
- Joseph was an ex-convict who became the greatest leader of his day.
- Moses had been a murderer, but God later spoke with him as a friend.
- Rahab had been a prostitute, but God forgave her and chose her to be an ancestor of Jesus.
- David had been an adulterer, but God set him as the standard for all righteous kings.
- Paul had been a religious murderer, a terrorist against God's people, but God transformed him into the greatest missionary in history.
- Mary Magdalene had been demon-possessed, but she was the first person to see the risen Christ and the one who bore the news to the disciples.
- Zacchaeus had been a cheater and a liar and a thief, but God so transformed him that he became one of

the most generous individuals to ever live in that
country.

- The entire church at Corinth had been filled with the
sexually immoral, idolaters, adulterers, male prosti-
tutes, homosexual offenders, thieves, people driven
by greed, drunkards, slanderers, swindlers. But Paul
said, "You were washed, you were sanctified, you
were justified in the name of the Lord Jesus Christ
and by the Spirit of our God" (1 Cor. 6:11).

All these folks had two things in common. First, they all
had a past, just as we do, and second, they had all been
seized, taken hold of, by God's grace—just as we can be.

There *is* power to conquer your past. When you realize
that God has taken hold of you in spite of your past, and that
all He asks of you in return is that you take hold of Him, you
can run the race, as Paul said, with perseverance. You can run
and not grow weary, as the writer of Hebrews said. You can
face a future free of your past.

And you can press on to win the prize of knowing Him
and becoming like Him and living with Him forever.

There is power to conquer your past!

# POWER TO CONQUER ANGER 5

**WHAT** comes to mind when you see the word *anger?* What images do you see? Does the word hit a nerve? Does it bring back dark memories? What does *anger* mean to you?

You may have heard the story about the little girl who asked her daddy, "What's the difference between anger and rage?"

The dad thought a moment and then responded, "Well, it's really a matter of intensity. Here, let me illustrate it." So he picked up the telephone, dialed a random number, and asked, "Is Melvin there?"

The man on the other end of the phone replied, "There's no Melvin here.

You ought to check your number before dialing." And he hung up. So the dad repeated the call, asked for Melvin again, and the man said, "You just called this number. There is no Melvin here. Don't call me again."

The dad said to his daughter, "See, that man's a little angry. He's upset. Now watch this." He dialed the number again and asked, "Is Melvin there?"

The man said, "You've called here twice already. You already asked if Melvin was here. I'm telling you, there's no Melvin here! You've got the wrong number!" Slam.

"You see, now he's angry," the dad said, "but watch this." He picked up the phone and dialed the same number one more time. "Hey, this is Melvin. Have there been any calls for me?" Then he held the phone away from his ear, looked at his daughter, and said, "Honey, *that's* rage."

So what comes to your mind when you think of anger? Certain people? Places? A particular situation? A recurring experience? Times when you blew up and kicked a door in or threw a chair or otherwise exploded?

Anger has a way of putting us in turmoil. It causes us, as they say, to put our mouth in motion before we put our mind in gear. It can alienate us from our friends and from our family. It can negatively affect almost every area of our life.

According to one study, one out of every five Americans has an anger management problem. According to FBI statistics, there were over 23,000 homicides in 1994 and 28 percent of those were caused by arguments occurring in the home—28 percent of the homicides due to domestic violence compared to only 7.6 percent that were gang related. Anger resulting in violence is the reason given for 22 percent of divorces in middle-class marriages.[4]

In researching this topic, I discovered a Web site specifically designed to give people an opportunity to vent their anger. Users can submit anything they wish about anyone they wish on this Web site. Incidentally, I would not recommend visiting this site—it's pretty ugly! I saw some of the entries and exited immediately. Very disturbing!

Someone has even created a CD to hypnotize people to treat their anger. I've been trying to figure out whether it's supposed to hypnotize me so I don't get angry or hypnotize someone else so they don't make me angry. Maybe it could help me with my golf game.

If there are so many people making money off of other people's anger, there must be a lot of angry people in this world.

So how do we deal with our anger? Can Jesus Christ give us the power to conquer anger?

In the Book of Ephesians, Paul is writing a letter to the church at Ephesus. In chapter 4, verses 26-27, Paul says, "In your anger, do not sin. Do not let the sun go down while you are still angry, and do not give the devil a foothold." Those are two good verses to put to memory. They apply to much of our lives.

Let's take a look at the definition of *anger*, the stages of anger, and the sources of anger. It's good to understand these issues as we seek biblical guidance in dealing with anger.

MedicineNet.com defines anger as "an emotional state

that varies in intensity from mild irritation to intense fury and rage. Anger has physical effects; it raises the heart rate and blood pressure and the levels of adrenaline and nonadrenaline."[5]

Anger involves our emotions. The anger Paul is addressing in these verses deals with violent passion, fury, and rage. *Webster's Dictionary* says that anger is "a feeling of displeasure resulting from injury, mistreatment, opposition . . . usually showing itself in a desire to fight back at the supposed cause of this feeling."[6] Anger is an emotional reaction of hostility.

## ANGER INVOLVES OUR EMOTIONS.

We know what anger looks like, and most of us know what anger feels like—from both sides. Have you ever been mad at something or someone? Can you remember a time when someone was mad at you? You know the feeling—you're trying to figure out where you should go and what you should do next. You even want to ask the dog where he hides when he's in trouble for something he did. Have you ever been on anger's receiving end?

Sometimes we determine that the source of our anger is another person. We tell ourselves, "Well, if I can just avoid that other person, I can avoid being angry."

Sometimes we decide that certain circumstances are at the root of our anger. We think, "I'm not mad at anybody. I'm just mad at the situation." Have you ever said that?

Or sometimes we're angry at groups of people. We create stereotypes, we lump a group of people all together, and that's where we get racism and, ultimately, hate crimes. That's also at the root of the terrorism of our day. Certain Islamist extremists have grouped all Americans together as the "enemy," and they're angry at all of us. They consider us the source of their problems and are lashing out violently at random groups of people.

Then there are people who aren't angry at other people, they're not angry at their situation, and they're not angry at groups of people. They're angry at themselves for their own actions or their own habits. Their inner guilt has boiled up into an overwhelming anger.

But real anger has a deeper root than any of these causes. Anger comes from *unmet expectations* of people, circumstances, ourselves, the church—or even God.

Think about it for a moment. Think about a time when you were mad at someone. You expected that person to act in a different way than he or she did, and so you got mad. Or you expected a person to respond in a certain way to something and he or she didn't and so you became angry. So what causes anger? Unmet expectations.

A situation, a circumstance, didn't turn out the way you thought it would, as you expected it to, and you became angry. It's a case of unmet expectations.

After doing something you wish you hadn't, you tell yourself, "I expected better of myself than to act that way. I should have known better. How could I have been such a fool?" Again, it's a matter of unmet expectations.

This happens even in the church. I've met the children of pastors who refuse to even step inside a church building because the way the church treated their families did not meet their expectations. Besides pastors' kids, there are many—too many—who feel as though the church mistreated them or their families. This is not what they expected from the church. Right or wrong, legitimate or not, when expectations are unmet, the result is anger.

Then, to further complicate the issue, we assume from our church culture that we're not supposed to get angry with God. Again, this idea comes from our church culture, not from the Bible. Scripture allows us the opportunity to talk with God about our anger—even our anger with Him.

Has God ever disappointed you? Has God ever not met your expectations? Now, you can be really spiritual and answer, "No, I've never felt as though God has let me down." But what about those times when you were praying about something and you wanted God to answer your prayer in a certain way, and He didn't do it your way? See, in much of our Christian culture, we're caught because we think we can't tell God we're mad at Him. If you read the Psalms, you'll see that you can be very honest with God about all of your feelings. But too often all of our unmet expectations gradually build up and before long we're living with deep-seated, ongoing anger.

Someone came up with a little acronym to deal with anger: AHEN. *A* stands for *anger*, which can be traced back to *hurt*, which comes from *expectations* that are unmet, which can be traced back to a perceived *need*, real or not. We determine we have a need, expect that need to be met, perceive that the need won't be met in a particular way, and then feel hurt. That hurt begins to fester, and the final result is anger.

It all adds up. You can trace it back each time you find yourself angry. You can ask yourself, "OK, why am I angry?" If you think it through and analyze your feelings, you'll eventually begin to recognize expectations that were unmet.

Were the expectations reasonable? Were your expectations justified? Did you have the right to expect certain consequences? We'll consider those issues a little later.

Let's first take a look at the five stages of anger. The first stage of anger is *mild irritation*. The irritation may be rather innocent. It may be just a feeling of discomfort or discontent brought about by something you weren't expecting. It may be something someone does that simply annoys you. You probably think, "Well, I'll get over it." Can you think of some things that just irritate you? We all have them and, at this stage, they're usually no big deal.

The next stage is *indignation*. Indignation is a feeling that whatever occurred has to be answered. It's a feeling that you can't just sit there—you need to do something. You feel the inner urge to express your resentment at the offense. You don't necessarily *do* anything; you just have a feeling that there ought to be some sort of response to a wrongdoing. That's indignation.

This can lead to the third stage of anger, which is *wrath*.

This stage of anger involves actual expression. Each of the first two stages is an intense emotion. In the third stage the emotion leads to action. So now you have to do something about the feeling. You may slam doors. You may bang your fists. You may kick the car or the mower, the dishwasher or the dog. You may yell and scream. But there is a point at which you put action behind the feeling. The anger has progressed to wrath.

Then, there's the fourth stage—*fury*. Fury is characterized by violence, a loss of emotional control. If you are a golfer, this is where you break the club. This stage is where you resort to intensified verbal abuse, physical attack, or loss of restraint.

While we were on vacation, my brother, my son, my dad, and I were out on the driving range just for a little while and we saw this guy. He was so proud of the new driver he had just bought for $400—I know because we could hear him telling his buddies how much it had cost. While he was hitting, he was saying, "Ooo, I like my driver. Ooo, I like my driver. Ooo, I am so good." I was watching him and thinking, "Well, you're not as good as you think you are." But he just kept swinging and putting on his show. His group teed off ahead of us. About halfway through the course I saw a club go flying over into the woods. That was the $400 driver he had just bought. No one in his right mind would take four $100 bills and throw them in the woods. You just don't do that. This guy had lost control of his actions. That's fury.

Fury can lead to the next stage—*rage*. This fifth stage of anger results in the temporary loss of sanity. This is the stage where people might commit murder. This is the stage where people do things they don't even realize they are doing; they have crossed over the line into this area of rage.

So if anger goes unchecked or continues to build, *mild irritation* leads to *indignation,* which leads to *wrath,* which leads to *fury,* which ends in *rage.*

What does the Bible have to say about anger?

The first thing that I notice from Scripture, interestingly enough, is that anger is a God-given emotion. Look at what Paul says in Eph. 4:26: "In your anger do not sin." *In your anger.* I don't think God is saying through Paul, "I don't want you to be angry, but I'll tolerate it. That's a negative emotion, but I'll tolerate it." I don't believe God says that to us.

Some people struggle with the idea that Christians have these intense emotions. But you and I were created as emotional beings. We have an emotional component that permeates our lives, and we experience the full range of emotions: joy, compassion, pain—and anger. If you begin in the Old Testament and search the Bible through the New Testament and the life of Christ, you will find God—the Father, Son, and Holy Spirit—dealing with all the emotions from joy to anger. The Bible tells us that God is "slow to anger." It does not say He does not get angry, but rather that He is slow to anger. We hear the phrase "sinners in the hands of an angry God." God has these emotions, and we are created like Him. We have intense emotions and we can't deny them. Anger is a God-given emotion. The Greek phrase literally reads "be angry"—"do not sin."

A second observation from this scripture is that anger is

not necessarily sinful. "In your anger do not sin." That is an imperative, a command. Paul is telling us, "When you're angry, do not sin." That's a key point. If the stages that I've mentioned are accurate, then our anger can reach levels where our actions are not Christlike. They are in no way whatsoever like Christ. So we need to understand this guideline: in our anger, we are still to be like Jesus Christ.

Was Jesus ever really angry? Of course He was. Consider the scene of Jesus throwing the moneychangers out of the Temple (see Matt. 21, Mark 11, and John 2). He was not in either the fury or the rage stage; His behavior was not out of control. He had not temporarily lost His sanity. He was most likely in the wrath stage, because He obviously felt like something ought to be done, so He did it; He expressed His anger in action, in activity. And so we see Jesus, in a controlled way, indicating, "Something ought to be done about this. My house is to be a house of prayer, but you have made it into a den of thieves. No longer is it going to be a den of thieves—not while I'm here and while I can do something about it." And so He fashioned a whip—sounds pretty angry to me—and began to drive them out. He saw innocent people being taken advantage of by those moneychangers, and He said, "This is going to stop. My house will only be used for its original purpose."

Paul got angry. In Gal. 5 Paul was dealing with a group of people who had decided that all of the Gentile Christians would need to follow Jewish Law in order to be truly Christian. Paul was preaching the doctrine of grace, and he got angry with the legalistic people.

If you read Paul's writings about people being divisive in the church, you really can't read those words passively. Paul said, "Get them out!" Why was he so angry and adamant about division in the church? Because Paul knew that unity had to exist in the church for it to be the Body of Christ.

Are there times when anger is appropriate? Yes. There are times when anger not only is not sinful but is truly appropriate. So when the kingdom of God is being damaged, are you supposed to run into the middle of it and lose control of your temper and your actions? No, there's never a place, time, or situation in which it is appropriate to lose control and act contrary to the character of Jesus. However, there are times when the emotion of anger should well up into action and we should do something about a situation.

Look at what Paul is saying in Eph. 4:26-27. Not only is anger a God-given emotion, not only is anger not necessarily sinful, but anger must also have boundaries. "Do not let the sun go down while you are still angry, and do not give the devil a foothold." There are two boundaries in this scripture. One is a *time boundary;* you must confront your anger. Sometimes we think if we get through the crisis and the emotion has subsided, then we've dealt with the anger. But the passing of the moment and the cooling of the temper do not necessarily mean we've dealt with our anger. The anger may be bottled up; we may have buried it. But the anger is still there. We haven't confronted it. We may have to go to the person with whom we're angry and deal with it, and we need to deal with it in a timely fashion. Don't just let the sun go down, and go down, and go down again. We need to confront our anger in good time, sooner than later. Paul says to us, "Don't let the sun go down on your anger. Get busy dealing with it."

Then Paul indicates that there is a *righteousness boundary*, an integrity limit. He says, "Don't give the devil a foothold." When we have unresolved anger in our hearts, when we are not dealing with that anger and there is an unsettled conflict buried inside us, what we're doing is opening the door to sin; we're giving Satan an opportunity to work in our lives. He comes along and whispers things like, "Uh huh, see? She did that to you before." "They always treat you like this." "He doesn't care at all how this makes you feel. No real friend would do that." Or the accuser may say, on a deeper level, "God doesn't care about you. You wanted this so much and it didn't happen. You prayed for this and God didn't give it to you." The devil is not going to step in and say, "Yeah, things didn't turn out the way you wanted, but you can trust God anyway." That's not his language; that's not what he does. When we're angry and we don't deal with it, we give the devil a foothold. Satan begins to use the unresolved anger and its results to destroy us.

Understand this truth: Unresolved anger will destroy your soul. It will destroy your home. It will destroy your family. It will destroy your children. It will destroy everything good in your life. You have to confront and deal with your anger in a timely way, or it will eventually allow sin to consume you.

So how do we typically deal with anger? Or more accurately, how do we typically *avoid* dealing with our anger? What are the inappropriate ways in which we cope with our anger?

Some people simply deny their anger exists. Although this is emotionally and spiritually unhealthy, we Christians are notorious for pretending we're not angry. As I mentioned earlier in this chapter, many Christians are uncomfortable with the idea that anger not only is natural but also can even be God-given. So rather than admit we're mad about something, we pretend to be unfazed and unbothered. One of our favorite ways for denying it is to make it sound or look like something else. We use nice words like "righteous indignation." Have you ever used that phrase? "I'm not angry; I'm righteously indignant." We use words like *upset.* "No, I'm not mad; I'm just *upset.*" "I'm just *irritated.*" "I'm just *aggravated*"—that's my personal favorite. I probably use that one more than any of them—"not angry, just aggravated." But denying our anger doesn't make it go away; it just festers inside us, causing deep emotional turmoil.

# NO, I'M NOT MAD; I'M JUST UPSET.

When denying our anger doesn't seem to be working, we may begin to intentionally bottle it up. We acknowledge that we're annoyed, maybe even angry, but we decide that as long as we don't act on that feeling, everything will be OK. But while denying anger is emotionally unhealthy, bottling anger up is physically unhealthy; it can literally kill you. Repressed anger can lead to stomach ulcers, a weakened immune system, or irresponsible behavior.

In contrast, others unleash it, uncork it, just let it all out. Now, this is unhealthy for everyone else. So, how can we deal with anger in a healthy, productive, and Christian way?

Paul tells us that first of all we have to *'fess up*, or confess our true feelings. In Eph. 4:22, Paul is talking about being honest. He talks about "put[ting] off the old self, which is being corrupted by its deceitful desires." In verse 25, he says, *"Put off falsehood and speak truthfully* to [your] neighbor, for we are all members of one body" (emphasis added). We have to call it what it is; we have to admit our anger and say we're angry when we're angry. Now, once we're honest about our feelings, we can begin to deal with them. But if we never admit anger, if we keep it bottled up or deny it, we cannot truly *conquer* anger in our lives. We have to 'fess up to our true feelings and emotions. Throughout this passage, the idea of truth permeates all that Paul is saying. We must learn to speak the truth, especially when we're angry.

We were building a church at our first pastorate and the carpenter had messed up—and in a *big* way, it seemed to me. I realize now that it really wasn't that bad now that I understand Sheetrock and the building process. But we had to redo the Sheetrock. I was walking through the church building, and I was thinking, *This isn't right. This is absolutely not right.* I went home that day and I was aggravated—OK, so I was angry! I went home and told my wife, Karan, "I am so mad! He should not have done that! He should've known better!" Now that I have finally come to understand anger, I know what I was dealing with at that time. The root of my anger was an unmet expectation. I'd expected the carpenter and his team to do the job right, they didn't do it right, and I was angry about it.

Yet, the problem was not a big deal. I thought it was at the time. I knew it was at the time. But it really wasn't at all. Isn't that the way it goes? Sometimes the issues we think are huge are not really big at all—it's just that we didn't know all the facts. We thought we did, but . . . well, that's where maturity comes in.

We need to not only 'fess up but also *grow up*. Look at what Paul says in Eph. 4:20-24:

> You, however, did not come to know Christ that way. Surely you heard of him and were taught in him in accordance with the truth that is in Jesus. You were taught, with regard to your former way of life, to put off your old self, which is being corrupted by its deceitful desires; to be made new in the attitude of your minds; and to put on the new self, which is created to be like God in true righteousness and holiness.

Here's the point: It's time for Christians to grow up. Clearly there are some things we must put aside, some petty disagreements we need to ignore, and some conflicts about which we just have to say, "You know what, we just need to deal with this. This is just how it is." But Paul's whole issue here is about growing up—about putting off the old self and

**IT'S TIME TO EAT SOME MEAT.**

putting on the new self. Whatever that old self may be—an attitude, a habit, or an action—as God exposes it in our lives, we need to say, "Lord, here it is. I ask You to get rid of that old self so that I can put on the new self." That's what it means to be transformed into the image of Christ—to grow up in Christ. It doesn't matter how old you are or how long you've been a Christian, if you're spiritually only drinking milk, it's time to eat some meat.

So we have to 'fess up, and then we have to grow up and allow God to change us. Then, third, we have to *move up*. Proverbs 22:24-25 says, "Do not make friends with a hot-tempered man; do not associate with one easily angered, or you may learn his ways and get yourself ensnared." In other words, we need to look at our close relationships. If the people to whom we are close are in the habit of flying off the handle, if our close friends don't have control of their tempers, we need to be careful because we will become just like them. We need to move up; in other words, we need to choose and nurture relationships with people who are living a strong, Christian lifestyle that exhibits discipline, particularly in this area of anger.

This is good advice for teenagers. Peer pressure is a powerful thing when you're young and forming your personality and habits. And it's important for teens to be careful when choosing their friends, especially because of this whole temper issue.

So we need to 'fess up, grow up, and move up. Then we need to *speak up*. Ephesians 4:25 says, "Therefore . . . put off all falsehood and *speak* truthfully to [your] neighbor" (emphasis added). Verse 29 adds, "Do not let any unwholesome talk come out of your mouths, but only what is helpful in building others up according to their needs, that it may benefit those who listen." In verse 31, Paul talks about getting rid of slander. In all this Paul is dealing with the concept of communication, which means we need to speak up.

When someone does something that does not meet our expectation, and after examination we are sure that it was a legitimate expectation, we have a right and even a responsibility to go and talk to that person about the situation. What is not acceptable is for a break to occur in the relationship with the person, because the Word of God calls for us to be together and to be one in Christ. That is absolutely imperative!

I have never understood how Christians can avoid speaking to one another. It makes no sense to me. I've seen one person come in and sit on one side of the church while another person sits on the other side. Although neither has spoken to the other in years, they seem to think that behavior is all right with God. How can they believe that? How can they excuse that kind of behavior within the church body? It is unresolved anger. Don't get me wrong; I'm not saying you have to be best friends and go out to eat every time you get a chance. But unresolved anger should not be in our lives, especially when it begins affecting our behavior within the church body.

Remember we must 'fess up, grow up, move up, and speak up. But when we do speak up, we must keep a close check on our tongue. We need to watch what we say. We must cultivate honesty in communicating with other people without allowing anger to build up and boil over into our words and actions.

Then finally, we have to *give up*. Ephesians 5:1 says, "Be imitators of God, therefore, as dearly loved children and live a life of love, just as Christ loved us and gave himself up for us as a fragrant offering and sacrifice to God." We have to surrender. Surrender to what? Surrender to the situation? No. Surrender to God. If we are going to be what God wants us to be, we're going to need the power to conquer the anger. We're going to have to reach the place where we say, *God, here it is. I am mad about this. I am angry over this. I've examined why I'm angry, and it boils down to an unmet expectation, but I have to give this to You. I must surrender this to You. I can't keep this bottled up inside of me, so, Lord, if I need to go talk to somebody, I want to do it with a Christlike attitude of love. And, God, before I can go talk to this person with a Christlike attitude of love, please change my heart. I surrender to You my right to retaliate. I surrender to You my right to lash out, because You had a right, Jesus, to lash out at me, but instead of lashing out, You gave up that right for me.*

Do you see how it all works together? When I experience anger in my heart, I 'fess up, I grow up, I move up, I speak up, and most importantly, I give up—I surrender it all to the power of Jesus Christ for the transformation of my heart.

You may be dealing with anger even now. What do you think of when you hear the word *anger?* Somebody's face? Some situation? Your mom or dad or spouse or son or daughter or brother or sister? The church?

Or God? *God, You didn't heal my child. You didn't heal my spouse. You didn't heal my son or daughter. And, God, I prayed and I punched every spiritual button I knew to punch. You were still God. How dare You?*

We can express our anger toward God. But then we can eventually say, *But I know You are God. So in the midst of all of this, help me surrender so that I can trust You and treat other people with the love that Christ has shown toward me.*

Paul sums it up best when he writes, "Be imitators of God, therefore . . . and live a life of love, just as Christ loved us" (Eph. 5:1). That's what it all boils down to—being just like Jesus. I think that's the heart of what we call *holiness.*

Maybe the Holy Spirit has been speaking to you as you've read this chapter. Perhaps He's urging you to 'fess up, grow up, move up, speak up, and give up regarding a particular circumstance. Maybe He's saying, "This situation or this person or this event has produced an unmet expectation in your life, and it needs to be brought before Me and given to Me." Remember, God will help you. He stands ready and willing and abundantly able to give you the power to conquer anger.

If you feel in your heart you need to pray and submit the anger in your life to God, don't hesitate. Don't let the sun go down on your anger one more time. Don't wait another day for the devil to get a foothold. Seek the face of God.

# POWER TO CONQUER CRITICISM  6

"**STICKS** and stones may break my bones, but words will never hurt me." Ever heard that? Ever said that? Not true, is it?

Have you ever heard any of these?

- "He's hopeless!"
- "She's worthless!"
- "I can't believe he made that decision!"
- "I can't believe she thought that!"
- "What in the world were they thinking?"
- "I don't like the way they did that down there."
- "You did that wrong."
- "I don't like them at all."
- "Can you believe he said that?"
- "She is just not right."

Words, phrases—criticism—it seems that at the end of each critical statement there ought to be an exclamation point, because it's hard to receive or give it without any emotion involved. In fact we tend to call cool, calm-collected criticism by other names—analysis, critique, or constructive criticism. Do you know what the difference between constructive criticism and destructive criticism is? Constructive criticism is when you criticize someone else; destructive is when they criticize you. Criticism is not fun for anyone except maybe the people who give it. The writer of Ps. 64 understood how damaging words could be: "Hide me from the conspiracy of the wicked, from that noisy crowd of evildoers. They sharpen their tongues like swords and aim their words like deadly arrows. They shoot from ambush at the innocent man; they shoot at him suddenly, without fear" (vv. 2-4).

Criticism is a part of life. On occasion I will teach a seminar on leadership, and one of the truths I warn leaders about is that if you are a leader, criticism is going to be part of your life. The only way to avoid criticism is to say nothing, do nothing, and be nothing. Then someone will look around and catch you saying nothing, doing nothing, and being nothing and will criticize you for it. If you have a hard time dealing with criticism, either learn to handle it or don't lead. It's just that way.

I remember my first pastoral recall vote in my first church in Spartanburg, South Carolina. The system has now changed, but at that time congregations voted on pastors. First it was every year; then when you're ordained, it was every two years. And if they really loved you, they could extend it to four, but they still voted. I remember the night before my first vote. I called my dad; he was a district superintendent of our denomination at the time, having served as a pastor for 20 years. I said, "Dad, I'm a little nervous. What if someone votes no tomorrow? What am I supposed to do?" He said, "Son, it'll be OK. Don't worry about it. In this day and age people might vote no." I probed a little deeper, "How did you handle it when you were a pastor?" Silence screamed at me through the phone, and finally he said, "I don't know. No one ever voted no on me." My rather emotional response was, "Can I speak to Mom? You're not much help. Thanks a lot."

Biblical characters faced criticism. There was Noah, Abraham, Jacob, Joseph, Moses, Joshua, David, the prophets, Daniel, John the Baptist, Jesus, Peter, Paul (and Mary), and the list could go on and on. Read their stories and you'll discover that they were criticized.

A child in a Sunday School class was asked, "Is there anything God cannot do?" To which he replied, "Yes! He cannot please everyone!" Even God has been the object of criticism. So how do we deal with criticism?

First, let's define it. According to the *Wordnet* dictionary, *criticism* can mean several things: "1. disapproval expressed by pointing out faults or shortcomings; 2. a serious examination and judgment of something; i.e. critique; 3. a written evaluation of a work of literature; i.e. literary criticism."[7]

In theology, higher criticism is a necessary discipline. But in relationships it is not. However, there are people who have refined the skill of criticism. Some do it so well that it seems to be a God-given gift! I'm not talking about higher criticism or literary criticism or a critique or analysis of something. I'm talking about criticizing people—definition No. 1 above—"disapproval expressed by pointing out faults or shortcomings."

So why do people criticize? I think there are four basic reasons. One is that people criticize in order to lift themselves up. It basically flows from insecurity. "Since I don't think I can get up to their level, I'm going to try to bring them down to mine." That's one reason criticism occurs. It's probably one of the two most common reasons, by the way.

A second reason people criticize stems from their own internal conflicts. When they are not at peace with themselves, when there is conflict going on *within* them, then people tend to lash out at others *around* them. If they're not happy with themselves, they're not happy with anyone else around them.

A third reason people criticize results from their being critical of the very thing for which they are guilty. When I've heard people criticize others, sometimes I want to tell them that they do the same thing themselves; they have the same attitude.

The fourth reason, and I think probably the most common, is that people criticize because they want control. They want to have the power to make adjustments in life and make decisions that will be best for them. When that doesn't happen, they resort to criticism. Sometimes people justify their controlling attitude by thinking that the issue at hand is nobler than what's best for them personally. Maybe they love the organization so much, whether it's the church or a business, that they become critical of others. They may even believe they have a right (and perhaps a responsibility) to criticize.

## BUT CRITICISM STINGS!

But criticism stings! It doesn't matter who you are or how tough you may be or how thick you make the façade, criticism stings. How do we handle it? What can we do as Christians to not only handle criticism but, if necessary, give it in constructive ways?

Look at Eph. 4:25—5:2. This particular passage of Scripture is in a letter Paul wrote to the church at Ephesus. Some believe it wasn't written just to the church in Ephesus but to all the churches of the region of Asia Minor. We do know it was at least circulated among the churches of that region. You can imagine someone standing before that gathering of believers and reading this letter from Paul.

> Therefore each of you must put off falsehood and speak truthfully to his neighbor, for we are all members of one body. "In your anger do not sin": Do not let the sun go down while you are still angry, and do not give the devil a foothold. He who has been stealing must steal no longer, but must work, doing something useful with his own hands, that he may have something to share with those in need.

Do not let any unwholesome talk come out of your mouths, but only what is helpful for building others up according to their needs, that it may benefit those who listen. And do not grieve the Holy Spirit of God, with whom you were sealed for the day of redemption. Get rid of all bitterness, rage and anger, brawling and slander, along with every form of malice. Be kind and compassionate to one another, forgiving each other, just as in Christ God forgave you. Be imitators of God, therefore, as dearly loved children and live a life of love, just as Christ loved us and gave himself up for us as a fragrant offering and sacrifice to God.

In this passage Paul's use of grammar is particularly important. The forms of the words and the words themselves indicate that the people in the church are supposed to stop doing something and start doing something else. Look at the scripture again and notice what he says. He talks about putting off falsehood; in other words, he's telling them to stop speaking falsely to one another and, instead, start speaking truthfully. He also tells them to stop stealing and start working. (And by the way, even working has a purpose—gaining wealth and resources to help people in need. Paul is constantly thinking beyond himself.) Then he tells them to stop talking unwholesomely and start building each other up with their words. They are to get rid of rage, slander, malice, brawling, bitterness, and so forth. And they are to start being kind and compassionate, forgiving of one another. Stop that and start this—that's his message to them.

When you read all of Paul's letters, you discover that one of the songs Paul likes to sing is the "no division among the people of God" song. Paul is mentally, emotionally, spiritually, physically, and relationally in total opposition to division in the church. Criticism is divisive. Criticism drains people of their energy. It steals their joy. It robs them of vision and makes them unproductive. Criticism is a major source of trouble for the church, and Paul has several ways of dealing with it.

Here are a few observations about criticism derived from Paul's thinking. First of all, *when we hurt others we hurt ourselves.* Hear again the words Paul wrote, "We are all members of one body" (v. 25). We may be arms, we may be feet, we may be hands, or we may be eyes, but we are all part of *one* body. There is a connection between criticizing others and damaging ourselves. One of the marks of the church is that we are a community of faith; we are the family of God. Whatever imagery you choose to use, whether it's the image of a team, of a family, or of a community, the fact is we are all connected. We are all one. It is also true that we are not the head of the Body. There is only one Head and that is Jesus Christ. We all belong to Him, and so we are all intricately connected to one another.

When we begin to criticize one another, we begin to hurt the Body as a whole. Think about this from the medical perspective. There is an entire series of diseases known as autoimmune diseases. For example, diabetes, lupus, alopecia (your hair falls out in round circles) are all autoimmune diseases. The doctors tell us that with these diseases the body actually attacks itself and starts shutting itself down. Think about how much this is like the way churches are all across the world—they actually begin to turn against themselves and shut themselves down. They render this arm useless; they terminate this leg; they stop those whose hands are touching the world. They shut down parts of the Body of Christ through critical words. When we hurt others, we hurt ourselves.

Second, *the devil gains an opportunity to divide and conquer when we behave wrongly.* That's what Paul is saying, "In your anger"—that particular word for anger means "provoked"—"do not sin." Then he says to "not let the sun go down while you are still angry" (v. 26). The word for "angry" here is a stronger word than the one he just used—it refers to rage. Then he says, "don't give the devil a foothold" (v. 27). In essence, when we don't behave or speak as we should, we create an opportunity for the devil to go to work in the organization, in the church, in the family, or in whatever other context there might be. In fact, an early Christian leader, Marius Victorinus, said, "We ourselves remain responsible for what we allow the devil to do in us." He doesn't have to gain a foothold, but if we're not careful, we can give him the opportunity to get one. Criticism tills the soil for anger and bitterness, which gives the devil the very foothold he wants.

Third, *God is distressed and saddened with our uncontrolled tongue and critical spirit.* In verses 29-30 Paul writes, "Do not let any unwholesome talk come out of your mouths, but only what is helpful for building others up according to their needs, that it may benefit those who listen. And do not grieve the Holy Spirit of God, with whom you were sealed for the day of redemption." It's a continual thought. When un-wholesome, rotten, worthless, disgusting talk comes out of our mouths and is directed toward others, God is saddened; He's grieved; He's distressed. Words that come out of our mouths should confirm, edify, and build up. God is simply not happy with a critical spirit in anyone.

In the Old Testament, Moses was often the object of criticism. Numbers 12 tells what happened when Miriam and Aaron, Moses' older sister and brother, criticized him. There was a little in-law spat going on, and they didn't like Moses' wife, so they criticized him because of her. So what did God do? He came down and said to Moses, Miriam, and Aaron, "Meet me at the Tent of Meeting." Now I don't know how they felt at that moment, but I do know how queasy I felt when I was a kid and had done something wrong and my dad would say, "Meet me in the living room in five minutes; we're going to have a conference." To this day, I still don't like to go to conferences.

Now God's meeting with Miriam, Aaron, and Moses was like my dad's conference with me—it was a one-way street. He did the talking, and they did the listening. God said to them, "When a prophet of the LORD is among you, I reveal my-self to him in visions. I speak to him in dreams. But this is not true of my servant Moses; he is faithful in all my house. With him I speak face to face, clearly and not in riddles; he sees the form of the LORD. Why then were you not afraid to speak against my servant Moses?" (vv. 6-8). In essence, God was saying, "Who do you think you are to criticize Moses?" What God did next really drove His point home. As soon as He finished chastising them and withdrew the cloud of His presence, Miriam looked down at her body and discovered she was covered with leprosy. Moses immediately began to intercede for her in prayer, and God heard him. But as a consequence for Miriam's critical spirit, God required her to live with the leprosy in isolation for seven days before being healed and restored to the community.

Do you think God is serious about criticism? You better believe it. Are you as thankful as I am for His patience? I would hope so. The fact is, we've all received criticism and we've all given it. There are times when the Holy Spirit has convicted us of criticism and we've had to repent. I'm sure there have been other times God has convicted us of criticism and we've ignored Him.

Fourth, *God instructs us regarding His expectations.* The entire portion of Paul's letter to the Ephesians that we are looking at is instruction. Rather than presenting a great new theological concept, Paul is taking the great theological principle of love and applying it to everyday life. This is what love looks like dressed up in work clothes every single day: we are to watch what we say, be careful of our feelings, deal with our thoughts, and be particularly careful about not letting our words express a critical spirit toward other people. Paul is encouraging us to speak words that are kind and sympathetic. What's more, if you notice, he is actually modeling what he's encouraging us to do. He's telling us not only what to stop but also what to start.

Now there are times and situations when we need to talk to a counselor or a pastor about relational issues, but that is not what Paul is writing about here. He is dealing with old-fashioned slander and gossip.

Sometimes when I become critical over an issue, the Holy Spirit will remind me that I really don't have a right to tear another person down. After all, I have enough things to be concerned about without criticizing others. Clearly we don't want to become dysfunctional in our communication by not addressing issues that need to be addressed, but a critical spirit is not acceptable before God. Paul models an approach for dealing with important issues while not giving in to a critical spirit.

Fifth, *God models His expectation for us.* All the way through this section of Ephesians Paul is saying implicitly what he writes explicitly in verse 32: "Be kind and compassionate to one another, forgiving each other, *just as in Christ God forgave you*" (emphasis added). He continues in 5:1-2, "Be imitators of God, therefore, as dearly loved children and live a life of love, *just as Christ loved us and gave himself up for us*" (emphasis added). God is saying, "I'm not asking you to do something I don't do. I'm asking you to imitate Me. As I am patient with others, as I try to build others up, while not ignoring the issues that must be addressed, you do the same. Yet, as you live this out in everyday life, do it in the right way, in the spirit of love. Follow My example."

Now the question to ask is not, "Will I or will I not be criticized?" but rather, "How can I handle criticism constructively?" A lot of literature has been written by counselors, psychologists, ministers, and others on how to handle criticism. They say things like this:

- Understand the differences between destructive and constructive criticism.
- Keep your own attitude in check.
- Look at the big picture.
- Take the high road of integrity.

**WE NEED TO BE UP FRONT WITH PEOPLE.**

Now those things are useful and similar to what Paul says. But for our purposes, it's best to understand what Paul actually does say about responding to criticism. Whether we are giving, receiving, or addressing criticism, the first step he gives us is to *"speak the truth in love"* (see 4:15, 25, emphasis added). We need to put off falsehood and get real. We need to be up front with people.

The second step is to *not be reactionary or emotion-driven.* "Don't let the sun go down while you are still angry" (v. 26). When we are angry, we must avoid mulling things over and over in our minds and spirits; instead, we should take action—but action that is thoughtful and collected.

The third step is found in verse 29, and that is to *build each other up.* We must determine not to stoop to the level of the critic. Most critics try to tear down, but we are to build up. This is one of the ethics of the kingdom of Christ. Christians should not be in the demolition business. That is not what God came to do. That's not why Jesus died on the Cross. The business of Christians is construction—the building up of one another.

Remember the scene painted so beautifully for us in Heb. 12? What do you think the people seated in the stands of eternity—that stadium filled with those who have completed their earthly race and are now watching us run our race—are saying? They're not shouting, "I can't believe that's how you're running your race! Boo! You're doing it all wrong!" No. The Word says they are cheering us on. They're encouraging us. That's the picture Paul gives us in Ephesians—a picture of people pulling for one another, building one another up.

The fourth step is to *not be defensive*. We need to stop focusing on ourselves and start looking at the needs of others. That's a strong statement. I have the basis for it, verse 29, underlined in my Bible. In fact, I have this entire section underlined in my Bible, but when it gets to the two words "their needs," it's underlined twice. They jump out at me.

The focus is on *their needs*, and as the verse says, we need to use our words to build others up according to what *they* need, not according to what *I* need. Then those who listen will receive benefit. Instead of being defensive, we need to look at the situation and ask, "What can I do to help them? What can I do to build them up?"

The fifth step is plain and simple: *"be kind and compas-*

*sionate*" (v. 32). Although that's self-explanatory and straight-forward, it can be difficult at times.

The last step is to *be gracious and forgiving* (see v. 32). You have received grace; be gracious. You have been forgiven; forgive.

Finally, in 5:1-2 Paul sums things up. As we've seen earlier, these verses tell us to be imitators of God and live a life of Christlike love. So what does that tell us about handling criticism constructively? It tells us that we do it through love. We are to love the criticizer, love the one who enjoys pointing out our faults. The power to conquer criticism is found in the power of God's love.

Sticks and stones may break my bones—and words do indeed hurt me, but instead of throwing the sticks and stones back at the criticizer, I can conquer the criticism with the power of God's love. I can do it because the Holy Spirit lives within me and He can do it through me. That's where the real power to conquer comes from—not from ourselves but from the Holy Spirit who is in us. So let's pick up the sticks and stones and build a house of love.

# POWER TO CONQUER FAILURE 7

**HAVE** you ever failed at anything? Have you truly and utterly failed at something you wanted to accomplish? Do you know the kind of failure I'm talking about?

Let's begin by defining *failure*. According to the *American Heritage Dictionary*, failure is "the condition or fact of not achieving the desired end or ends: *the failure of an experiment* ... the condition or fact of being insufficient or falling short: *a crop failure* ... a cessation of proper functioning or performance: *power failure* ... nonperformance of what is to be requested or expected ... : *failure to report a change of address* ... a decline in strength or effectiveness."[8]

"The inability to function or perform satisfactorily," "a lack of success," "falling short"—any of those things hit home to you the way they hit home to me? However we define it or whatever words we use, we intrinsically know what failure is because we have been there.

Even people associated with success have been considered failures at one time or another. How about Henry Aaron? We wouldn't consider Henry "Hammering Hank" Aaron a failure, would we? Hammering Hank was one of my childhood heroes, with 755 home runs. But did you know he struck out 1,383 times? You'll find that in the stats. Almost 1,400 times he stepped up to the plate and failed to get a hit or hit a homerun—or even get on base!

What about Vincent Van Gogh? We wouldn't consider him a failure, would we? But the masterful painter sold only one painting while he was alive.

Abraham Lincoln is one of the greatest American presidents ever. In fact, some of us would consider him *the* greatest. But he is also one of the greatest examples of failure. Students of American history know his story. He dropped out of grade school to run a country store. He failed at business twice. It took him 15 years to get out of debt. He lost his bid for U.S. representative twice. He ran for the U.S. Senate twice and lost twice. Altogether, he lost eight elections. He had a nervous breakdown. He delivered a now-famous speech to an indifferent crowd. He was attacked daily by the press, was despised by half the country, and finally was assassinated. But was Abraham Lincoln a failure? He may have failed on occasion, but we would not call him a failure. He once said, "My great concern is not whether you have failed, but whether you are content with your failure."

The average entrepreneur fails 3.2 times before achieving success. William Ward once said that adversity causes some men to break and others to break records.

Let's switch our focus to Scripture. The Bible is full of people who have failed because the Bible records life as it is. So we can talk about famous failures even in Scripture.

Consider Jacob. We know Jacob as the father of the 12 sons for whom the tribes of Israel are named. We know Jacob as the man who spent the night wrestling with the Lord. When you talk about a prayer warrior, someone who hangs on to what he or she believes, and a person who holds on to the Lord, you can always use Jacob as an example. But as recounted in chapter 3, before his great change of heart, Jacob had deceived his father, stolen his brother's inheritance, and despised his first wife, Leah.

What about Moses? We all know the story of Moses, that he was the great individual whom God used to lead His people out of captivity and raise up a nation. We know, too, that Moses was the great lawgiver. In fact, our law and the laws of one civilization after another for thousands of years were based on what he wrote down. But we also are aware that Moses was a murderer and someone who fell short—a failure.

Another great example of failure would be David. You know who King David was. He was the king who was the model for all good kings. In fact, you can read many passages in the Old Testament, and if the subject is a king who was a righteous king, it says, "he walked in the steps of King David," "he followed King David," or "he followed his father David," because David was the model for all great kings. But David had the husband of his mistress killed. And when he stood beside the grave of his dead infant, he stood there as a total moral failure.

How do people recover from this kind of failure? Where do we find God when we fail? Someone once said that most of us never see God in our failure but only in our success. What an ironic attitude for people who have the Cross as the center of their faith.

Let's consider the failure of Peter. The story begins following the Last Supper, during the evening before Jesus was betrayed and seized, tried, and crucified. Jesus said to His disciples, "You will all fall away" (Mark 14:27$a$). In other words, you will all fail. Then Jesus continues, "For it is written, 'I will strike the shepherd, and the sheep will be scattered.' But after I have risen, I will go ahead of you into Galilee.' Peter declared, 'Even if all fall away, I will not.' 'I tell you the truth,' Jesus answered, 'today—yes, tonight—before the rooster crows twice, you yourself will disown me three times'" (vv. 27$b$-30).

Do you hear how direct that is? "You yourself." No wonder Peter never asked, "Who, me?" But he still insisted emphatically, "Even if I have to die with you, I will never disown you" (v. 31). And all the others said the same thing. Can't you just hear the crowd? "Not me, Lord, not me! I'm not going to fail You. I'm not going to disown You. They may come and they may arrest You and do whatever else, but I'm not going to disown You, because I don't care who knows. I'm not ashamed to be Your disciple, and I'm going to stand up for You—even if it costs me my life!"

Let me give you some failure myths before we take a closer look at this passage. These are some things that people believe about failure that are simply not true. One myth is that failure is avoidable. It's not. Some things are avoidable, but not failure. You can count on failure as being a fact of life. It's going to happen, no matter what.

## FAILURE ISN'T FINAL.

Another myth is that failure is a particular event. If you get an F on a report card, it doesn't mean that you failed one specific event or activity. That grade indicates your failure to learn a given subject. True failure is a condition.

A third myth is that failure is irreversible. It's not. Our problem comes when we confuse *failing* with *failure*. They are two different things.

Another myth closely connected with the previous is that failure is final. It does not have to be final—not if we recognize that everyone experiences failure and that God's love and forgiveness are not dependent upon our success. Failure isn't final if we learn to grow from our failures and if we allow ourselves to put our failures behind us.

You see, failure takes many forms. Sometimes failure

comes as disappointment. Have you ever been disappointed —especially in yourself? Failure may come as a result of a friend or partner letting us down. It may come because our child has taken the wrong road in life or a mate has been unfaithful. It may even come because we have messed up and we see our own failure. All of us have experienced failure in some way.

Hear the declaration of Peter in Mark 14:29: "Even if all fall away, I will not." Now let's fast-forward past his failure, past Jesus' resurrection. In John 21 we find Peter and the disciples talking, saying to each other, "What are we going to do now?" Peter says—and I'm paraphrasing here—"I don't know about you guys, but there's one thing I know how to do: I know how to fish. When nobody else can catch fish, I can. I know where the fish are, I know how to get them, and that's what I'm going to do—go fishing." The rest of them decide to do the same thing and go fishing too. So they go out and get in the boat and are out all night long—and they catch nothing. This letdown complicates Peter's sense of failure: "Well, I thought I could fish, but I must have lost my touch. I thought I was good at this, but I guess I'm not. It looks like I've failed again."

So what do we do when this happens to us? How should we deal with failure? Allow me to make a few observations.

First, God is not surprised when we fail. Look at what Jesus says to Peter (paraphrased): "You're going to deny Me. All of you are going to fail Me. All of you are going to fall away." Peter protests, "Not me. No, I'm not." Jesus responds, "Yes, you are. In fact, before the rooster crows twice, you will fail Me three times." And sure enough, Peter fails and God is not surprised. When Jesus and Peter see each other again and their eyes meet, Peter is looking for a "See? I knew it!" kind of thing in Jesus' eyes. But in His eyes, Peter only sees grace. He sees forgiveness.

So why is God not surprised when we fail? Is it because of His foreknowledge, or is it because He knows we're human and humans are going to mess up when we rely on our own strength? I'm not sure, but for whatever reason, God is not surprised.

The second observation is that no one really wants to fail. Again, in Mark 14:29 Peter in essence says, "I will not deny You!" And then verse 31 states, "But Peter insisted emphatically, 'Even if I have to die with you, I will never disown you.'" Notice the word *emphatically*. It is inserted because in the Greek his statement is in the emphatic form. Peter is saying it with the strongest language he can use: *"I will never disown you."*

No one sets out to fail. You don't go to school every single day or study just to get out of college to be a failure. You don't get up every day and go to work and put the time and energy into your job just so you can fail in your career. You don't teach your kids and try to live the right kind of life in front of them just so you can fail as a parent. No one *wants* to be a failure. And yet failure still seems to come our way.

Here's the third observation: Self-confidence is not enough to prevent or overcome failure. Peter said, "I will never disown you." Now, was Peter self-confident or what? Read the stories of Peter in the Gospels; time and time again, you will find Peter being outspoken and self-confident. When no one else would speak or before anyone had a chance, Peter would speak. Peter was the one who stood in the presence of God and "the big three" at the Transfiguration and said, "Let's build three tabernacles right here! That's what we need to do. We need to set up three churches right on this spot!" And God said, "Peter, be quiet." (See Matt. 17:4-5.) Self-confidence—Peter had it and of that there's no doubt. If anyone could, through self-confidence alone, avoid failure, Peter would have been the very one. And yet he failed.

So what does that leave us with? Do we give up? Some people do. Some people let the fear of failure keep them from eventual success. Keep this in mind: It's not what happens *to* you but what happens *in* you that matters most. And when you give up, you remove yourself from the growing process. Giving up should not be an option.

There are also people who lash out and lay blame. They blame the situation, blame other people, and blame everything and anything other than themselves.

Other people get down on themselves. They look at the failure and take responsibility for it, but then they sink into a depression and say, "Well, it's just me. I am a failure. I'll never succeed." That drives them into what we could call "Never, Ever Land." They say things like "I'll never, ever try something like that again" or "I'll never, ever take another risk like that." So they shut down and settle for less than their potential in Christ—all because they've experienced failure.

114

Now if you are thinking that surely there must be a better way to deal with failure, you are right. There is a better way, and it's found in Scripture.

If we want to deal productively with failure, the first thing we need to do is *own* it. It's essential that we admit our own failure. In Mark 14, we see Peter denying Christ. Here is a clear example of failure. Later, in verse 72, we find Peter weeping bitterly. Now I'm referring to the Gospel of Mark specifically because many historians tell us that Peter told his story to Mark; the Gospel of Mark is basically the Gospel of Peter. So here we have Peter—in essence recording his own story—saying, "I emphatically said that I would not deny Christ even if I had to die." He didn't say, "Well, I didn't think I would have to give up my life." He said emphatically, "I will not deny You even if it costs me my life." And he meant what he said. He knew he might have to give up his life. Yet, as the Gospel records, he does deny Christ. Upon hearing the rooster crow, he remembers the words of Christ and sits down and weeps. He is admitting to himself, "I have failed." He is taking responsibility for his failure.

That's what we have to do. If we're ever going to conquer failure in our lives, we have to reach that place where we own it, where we admit it. We have to realize that the failure is ours alone. No one else is to blame. And we can't just blame the situation. We each have to say, "It's my responsibility. I'm the one here who has to deal with my own failure." That's first and foremost.

Jesus talks about this in Luke 6, when He says, "How can you say to your brother, 'Brother, let me take the speck out of your eye,' when you yourself fail to see the plank in your own eye? You hypocrite! First take the plank out of your eye, and then you will see clearly to remove the speck from your brother's eye." In other words, Jesus is saying, "Look at your own life, look at your own failures, look at your own issues, and take responsibility for them." And we often respond, "But, Lord, that's not as much fun. I'd much rather tell others about their problems than deal with my own. I'd rather be a spiritual consultant." I wonder if I could start a firm like that—Spiritual Consultants, Inc. When you're a consultant, you don't have to live with the results. You just go in and tell someone, "This is how you do it," and if it doesn't work well, you can just collect your money and walk out. It's a lot easier to talk to somebody else about their problems than to deal with your own.

So the first step in dealing with failure is to take responsibility for it—to own it. The second step is to *submit* it.

Remember, Mark's Gospel is Peter's story, and Peter told Mark about Jesus' resurrection. He said that the women went to the tomb and the angels told them to go and tell the disciples the great news, the Resurrection news. Peter told Mark that the angel said, "Go, tell his disciples *and Peter*" (16:7, emphasis added). You won't find that in any other Gospel, but here you see it because Peter was saying, "It was for me"—just as it's for all of us, just as it's personal for every one of us. In other words, Peter had come to grips with his own sense of failure, but he had also come to grips with his being able to *submit* his failure to Christ upon His return.

In Matthew's Gospel, we find all the disciples bowing at the feet of Jesus, worshiping Him. So Peter had reached that place where he was able to say, "Lord, You know I have failed You. Yet You have offered grace and acceptance and mercy, and Your acceptance of me does not depend on my performing flawlessly."

# WE MUST OWN OUR FAILURE.

We often think that God is not going to accept us and that other people are not going to accept us because we have failed. So what must we do? We must own our failure, and we must submit it before God.

Some people might be inclined to say, "I don't know what you're talking about because I've never failed." Well, Rom. 3:23 says that we've all sinned and that we fall short of the glory of God. We *all* have failed, but are we willing to submit our failure to God and accept His grace? First John 1:9 says, "If we confess our sins, he is faithful and just and will forgive us our sins and purify us from all unrighteousness." If I confess my sins, I have to submit them—I have to give them to Him. And then what happens? The grace of God is ours in Christ Jesus.

So we own our failure, we submit it to God, and then, third, we *face* it. We have to face our failure head-on.

When we compare Peter before the Crucifixion with who

117

he was after Pentecost, we see a huge difference. He was a new man. He still had confidence, and he was still outspoken. Yet his confidence and his ability to speak now came from his reliance on Jesus Christ through the power of the Holy Spirit rather than through his own strength or stubborn will.

What Peter learned is very significant. Peter learned that failure may be a fact of life, but failure does not have to be a *way* of life. He was able to submit his failure to the Lord, he was able to face it, and he was able to adjust his expectations.

Perhaps we, too, need to adjust our expectations. What do I mean by that? Can we really expect instant perfection from past failures? Can we really expect to never fail again? No— probably not, but I'm not talking about deliverance from failure. I'm talking about making adjustments because of failure.

I play the trombone, and over the years I've had to learn a lot of licks. Licks are rifts, phrases, parts that you have to play but that you can't just sit down and play naturally the first time. You've got to work on them. When I was a kid, I used to go into our living room to practice the trombone. Along with a piano and furniture I was not supposed to sit on, the living room had a trombone stand and a music stand. So I'd stand in there and play a lick over and over until my parents were ready to go out of their minds. But I would just keep playing it until it finally clicked. Then I'd go, "Yeah, that's it! That's the way it's supposed to be played." But, you see, my expectation was to pick up the trombone and play the lick right off the bat. I had to learn to adjust that expectation.

Some things take a lot of work. Although the power of

God is able to deliver us from habits and addictions, there are some behaviors, some issues, some ways of living that we simply have to spend time changing and relearning. So maybe we have to adjust our expectations based, again, on the power and presence of God in our lives.

So we own it, we submit it, and we face it. We look at our failure and say, "I need the Holy Spirit to empower me to work on this."

Fourth, we let God *use* it—we let Him build on it. Believe it or not, a past failure can be used as the training ground for tomorrow's success. Tom Watson Sr., who founded IBM and guided that company for over 40 years, said, "You can be discouraged by failure, or you can learn from it. So go ahead and make mistakes, make all you can. Because, remember that's where you'll find success—on the far side of failure."[9]

**GOD WANTS TO USE OUR FAILURE.**

God wants to use our failure. He wants to redeem it so He can build on it and utilize it in our lives for greater success in the future—success defined as He defines it.

Failure can be a stepping-stone to a better place or a springboard to a higher plane. A friend of mine, John, a layman in a church I pastored, had had a failed business, but instead of living in that failure, he would say, "Failure is success under construction." Sure enough, by the time I was his pastor, John had a thriving business.

Now you may think I'm simply touting business principles here. But I'm not. I'm talking about something that goes deeper than that. I'm talking about how we live our lives in Christ.

Dr. Joyce Brothers said, "The person interested in success has to learn to view failure as a healthy, inevitable part of the process of getting to the top."[10] Now she's talking about business and the world's view of success, but it can also relate to succeeding in what really matters in life: allowing Christ to change us and transform us. We may fail along the way, but failure doesn't have to be final.

I look at Peter's failure and I see that he owned it, submitted it, faced it, and let God use it. But what made the real difference for him? Was it simply that he went through those four steps and everything turned out OK? No. There was something more at work here, something that went beyond this incident. Before the Crucifixion, Peter was someone who, in total self-confidence, said, "I will never fail"—but he failed. After Pentecost, the same man who had been so afraid for his life that he denied Jesus three times stood up to testify in front of a huge crowd. Peter began to proclaim to the people that there is only one name by which we can be saved— *Jesus*, the name of the Man the same crowd had crucified just a few weeks earlier.

What changed Peter into this new person? The difference was the Holy Spirit in his life. Peter brought his failure to the Lord, brought himself before the Lord, and said, "Here I am, God. Do something in me." He, along with the rest of Jesus' disciples, waited and prayed until the Holy Spirit came and filled his life, redeemed his failure, and brought him success—so much success that it cost him his life.

Did Peter ever fail again? Sure he did. When Peter, Paul, the Gentile church, and the Jewish church got together, they agreed that the Gentile Christians didn't have to follow the same rules that the Jewish Christians did. In fact, Paul said, "There is neither Jew nor Greek, slave nor free, male nor female, for you are all one in Christ Jesus" (Gal. 3:28). And the council in Jerusalem said, "We're not going to put any responsibilities on the Gentile believers except for a few minimum requirements. By grace you have been saved. This is the way we're going to live" (see Acts 15:8-9, 23-29). Then a group of Jewish Christians began putting pressure on Peter not to eat with the Gentiles. And even though Peter was the one who first carried the gospel to the Gentiles when he spoke with Cornelius (see Acts 10), he finally gave in to the peer pressure and walked away from what he believed about this matter; he made a wrong decision and failed. Paul then had to confront Peter and show him where he'd gone wrong. Peter realized what he had done and set about making it right.

You see, as Christians we may fail again. And when we do, we can once more take our failure and own it, submit it, face it, and let God use it, remembering all the while that it is the power of the Holy Spirit that helps us overcome and conquer failure in our lives.

What failure is holding you back now? Is it a failure from 20 years ago or one from yesterday? Are you struggling and trying to get past a habit, a thought process, or an addiction? Do you keep praying, *I will never do this again, Lord,* and yet find yourself in the same place again and again.

Perhaps now you're ready to say, "There is hope in the Holy Spirit, and if I will own my failure and submit it and face it and give it to God and rely on His Spirit, He'll transform it into something He can use."

Remember, there are a lot of things that will fail: our bodies, our cars, our computers, our jobs, our businesses, our government, our dreams and visions, other people, our children, our marriages, our relationships, and more will all fail. But there are also things that will never fail: God's Word, God's compassion, God's grace, God's strength, God's promise of eternal life, God's love. Most importantly, God will never fail. It's through Him—the God who never fails—that we who do fail are victorious.

# POWER TO CONQUER SELF

**8**

**A THEOLOGY** professor once asked his class, "What are sins of omission?" And a student raised his hand and said, "Aren't those the sins we should have committed but didn't?" Not exactly. But what do you do when sin tries to entrap you, when sin tries to ensnare you? What do you do when it tries to entangle you? Genesis 37 is a story about a man who was entrapped by sin. It's a story of intrigue and deception, hate, family violence and family division, jealousy and injustice, and sin. Sounds like a story out of the newspaper, doesn't it? As a matter of fact, if this story happened today, you would hear about it on every news channel from CNN to Fox. "Young man missing in Dothan, presumed killed by wild animals. Investigators are on the scene. Body still not located." It's an incredible story. Let me just summarize it for you before we go any further.

Ten brothers committed a violent act against an 11th brother. They hated him and seized him and sold him into slavery. He became a trusted servant to his owner, but later, after being falsely accused of an indiscretion with his owner's wife, was thrown into prison. Yet, after several opportune events, he was released from prison, gained the confidence of the king, and became the second most powerful person in the land. By now you've probably guessed who this story is about. This is the story of Joseph—a story that swings like a pendulum from privileged son to prisoner to powerful ruler. It's one of the most popular biblical stories of all time and has inspired songs, movies, and theater productions. Let's take a closer look at it and see what truths it has for us.

Jacob had 12 sons. The son he loved most was named Joseph, and Joseph suffered injustice at the hands of his brothers for three particular reasons. One reason was that he told the truth. In Gen. 37, Joseph was sent to find out how his brothers were doing. He found his older brothers goofing off, so he returned and told his dad what was going on. Well, no sibling likes to be ratted on by a brother or sister, right? Yet, Joseph reported on the conduct of his brothers—he told the truth. And his brothers hated him. Being committed to the truth will do that; it will inevitably alienate some people.

The second reason Joseph was hated by his brothers was because Joseph was Jacob's favorite child. It's quite evident in the story that Joseph was his father's favorite. Remember the richly ornamented robe Jacob gave Joseph but did not give the others. It wasn't Joseph's fault. Maybe in his immaturity Joseph did some things to capitalize on his favored status, but still, Jacob should have known better. In fact, Jacob knew what it was like not to be the favorite child of his father. His father always favored Esau, and so Jacob, of all people, should not have repeated the mistake his father made.

We see this occur too often today. A parent will do something his or her children despise, yet the children themselves, even when pointing out what they despised in their parents, will turn around and repeat that very action in their own lives. We have to be on guard; we have to be aware of that natural tendency. Jacob had fallen into that very trap, and Joseph's brothers deeply resented their father's favoritism toward him.

The third reason Joseph experienced injustice was because he was authentic and honest. Joseph was a dreamer, and he had very specific dreams. He dreamed his brothers would bow down to him and he would rule over them—a total departure from family and cultural tradition. That kind of respect would only have been shown to the eldest son, and Joseph was far from that. But those were his dreams, and he dared risk being vulnerable in telling them to his brothers. Sometimes our authenticity will make us vulnerable. At times it will cause people to abuse or dislike us.

So, for several reasons Joseph's brothers did not like him. In fact, they hated him.

Now, let's pick up the story in Gen. 37:

> Now his brothers had gone to graze their father's flocks near Shechem, and Israel said to Joseph, "As you know, your brothers are grazing the flocks near Shechem. Come, I am going to send you to them."
>
> "Very well," he replied.
>
> So he said to him, "Go and see if all is well with your brothers and with the flocks, and bring word back to me." Then he sent him off from the Valley of Hebron.
>
> When Joseph arrived at Shechem, a man found him wandering around in the fields and asked him, "What are you looking for?"
>
> He replied, "I'm looking for my brothers. Can you tell me where they are grazing their flocks?"
>
> "They have moved on from here," the man answered. "I heard them say, 'Let's go to Dothan.'"
>
> So Joseph went after his brothers and found them near Dothan *(vv. 12-17)*.

Shechem was about 50 miles from where Jacob and Joseph were living. And Dothan, almost in a straight line, was another 50 miles. So Joseph reached his brothers 100 miles from home. That doesn't sound like a great distance today except when we remember they were on foot. So they were a long, long way from home. The brothers saw him coming in the distance, and before he reached them, they plotted to kill him.

> "Here comes that dreamer!" they said to each other. "Come now, let's kill him and throw him into one of

these cisterns and say that a ferocious animal devoured him. Then we'll see what comes of his dreams."

When Reuben heard this, he tried to rescue him from their hands. "Let's not take his life," he said. "Don't shed any blood. Throw him into this cistern here in the desert, but don't lay a hand on him." Reuben said this to rescue him from them and take him back to his father.

So when Joseph came to his brothers, they stripped him of his robe—the richly ornamented robe he was wearing—and they took him and threw him into the cistern. Now the cistern was empty; there was no water in it.

As they sat down to eat their meal, they looked up and saw a caravan of Ishmaelites coming from Gilead. Their camels were loaded with spices, balm and myrrh, and they were on their way to take them down to Egypt.

Judah said to his brothers, "What will we gain if we kill our brother and cover up his blood? Come, let's sell him to the Ishmaelites and not lay our hands on him; after all, he is our brother, our own flesh and blood." His brothers agreed.

So when the Midianite merchants came by, his brothers pulled Joseph up out of the cistern and sold him for twenty shekels of silver to the Ishmaelites, who took him to Egypt.

When Reuben returned to the cistern and saw that Joseph was not there, he tore his clothes. He went back to his brothers and said, "The boy isn't there! Where can I turn now?"

Then they got Joseph's robe, slaughtered a goat and dipped the robe in the blood. They took the ornamented robe back to their father and said, "We found this. Examine it to see whether it is your son's robe" *(vv. 19-32)*.

How unfair! What injustice! What incredible treachery and phenomenal deceit! So many times we identify with Joseph. Right? I mean, we go through trials, difficulties, and hard times. We've been deceived, and people have not always treated us justly or fairly. We've made the right choices during difficult times and did the right things but still ended up in trouble, just as Joseph did when he landed in prison.

**WHAT INJUSTICE!**

Plus, Joseph's story didn't stop there. God eventually rescued him from prison, and Joseph ascended to power and became the second most powerful individual in Egypt (probably the whole world). And so, amid our own troubles, we rejoice, saying, "Yes! We're a lot like Joseph." We're waiting and hoping for the day when God will bring us out of our trials and tribulations too.

However, on this stage of scripture, as we view the cast of the "Joseph Goes to Egypt" story, let your eye scan the characters and then zoom in on Reuben. We're probably much more like Reuben than we'd like to admit. Reuben had the opportunity to do the right thing. He had the opportunity to make some right choices. Look at him closely.

What do we do when sin tries to entrap us, when sin tries to ensnare us, or when sin tries to entangle us? What kind of choices do we make? I think we can discover how to handle it right here in this story with Reuben.

Do you know what it's like to try to make difficult decisions and do the right things but not really get anywhere? Paul describes this beautifully in Romans: "I do not understand what I do. For what I want to do I do not do, but what I hate I do" (7:15). Isn't that the predicament we often find ourselves in?

Now let's look again at Reuben. Why didn't he do the right thing? Why didn't he stand up to his brothers? Maybe Reuben didn't have the *authority* to make a difference. Maybe he didn't have enough clout. Don't we feel that way sometimes? "Well, it's not my place. I don't have the authority. I don't have the position to stand up and say this is right or wrong, or this is the thing we should do." But in Reuben's case, he did have the authority. He was the oldest. He could have taken a stand and made a difference. He was in the right position.

Now you may be thinking, *Well, that's Reuben. In his case he was the oldest and he had the authority. That's different.* The truth is, we also have the authority. We also have the power. We're also in the right position. Jesus said in the Great Commission, "All authority in heaven and on earth has been given to me. Therefore go and make disciples" (Matt. 28:18-19). Jesus gave us authority. He sent us into the world *in His name.* So, the authority and power of Jesus has been given to us. That's why James said, "Submit yourselves, then, to God. Resist the devil, and he will flee from you" (James 4:7). You and I have power through the Holy Spirit, and we have the position as children of God to refuse the wrong and do the right. Reuben had the authority to make the right decision, so that wasn't his excuse.

Maybe Reuben didn't do the right thing because he was *afraid*. Maybe he was afraid to take a stand or to swim against the tide of immorality. Can you relate to that? Have you ever been there, afraid to speak up so you choose to be silent? Afraid to take the action for fear of rejection? Or could it be the fear of failure? Maybe that was Reuben's problem.

However, I don't believe such was the case. Reuben planned to sneak Joseph out of the cistern at night and then take him back to his father, telling his father how he, Reuben, had rescued Joseph. Reuben knew the other brothers would be out to get revenge for that action because Reuben would have made them look really bad. But Reuben didn't care how the others would respond. He wasn't afraid of them. I don't think fear was his motivation.

Fear may sometimes be our motivation, but it is not a legitimate motivation for us. When we are trying to decide about doing right and rejecting wrong, we may be afraid others will reject us and that we will end up standing alone. But through the Holy Spirit we don't have anything to fear. God's love will drive the fear away from us.

Well, maybe Reuben was *addicted to* giving in. Maybe he just always gave in and gave up. Maybe that was just normal for him; it was his modus operandi. Perhaps he would talk about what he shouldn't do, but then do it anyway.

If we have a habit of giving in to sin, if we have a record of past failures, is there any hope that we can overcome that pattern of behavior? Is there any possibility of changing this tendency toward caving in to sin? Absolutely!

The present work of God in our lives means the past does not have to determine the future. Hear that again: *The past does not have to determine the future.* Past failures do not have to be repeated. Habits can be replaced. Addictions can be broken. We would naturally think that if event *A* happens, then *B* is sure to follow and it will lead to *C*. However, God breaks in on this scene and declares that the past does not have to determine how we choose to behave in the future.

Every single one of us has sinned against God—for we "all have sinned and fall short of the glory of God" (Rom. 3:23). But that does not mean we have to continue to live in that predicament. Our past failures do not mean we have to continue to fail, because there is a power that will help us overcome sin and failures in our lives.

So, Reuben's record is irrelevant. Just because he failed in the past did not mean he had to fail this time. Reuben had no excuse.

So what was his motivation? What was it about Reuben that caused him to choose poorly and be entrapped by sin? Could it be that deep down Reuben would only do what was right *when it benefited Reuben?* The fact that it was the right thing to do wasn't enough to make him do it. It wasn't enough that the God of Abraham, Isaac, and Jacob was a righteous God. Instead, Reuben's only motivation for action was *selfishness*.

Here's what seems to have happened. First, Reuben planned on saving Joseph's life. He was going to get Joseph out of the cistern (which sounds real noble when you first read the story), and then they were going to return to their father at Hebron. Reuben would then tell his father, "Look, they were going to kill him, but I saved him. Now, will you make me a robe of many colors? Will you favor *me* now?" To see why this is a likely scenario, let's look at the actual story.

When Reuben finds out that Judah and the brothers have sold Joseph into slavery, look at what he says: "The boy isn't there! Where can *I* turn now?" (Gen. 37:30, emphasis added). Not "I wonder what's going on with Joseph" or "I wonder if the Ishmaelites are treating him right." Not "I wonder if his chains are too tight" or "I wonder if they're giving him enough to drink." And certainly not "I wonder if I can get the 20 pieces of silver and go back and free my brother."

None of these responses came from Reuben. Instead, he says, "Where can *I* turn now?" Can you see what is missing? There was no concern whatsoever for Joseph. It was all about *Reuben*. "What am *I* going to do now? *My* plans are foiled. *I* was going to get in good graces with my father. But, *I* can't do that anymore. They have ruined *my* plans. How could they do this to *me?*"

How do we get entrapped by sin? Ensnared by sin? Entangled into sin? Is it because we see everything from a selfish perspective? You see, *the real culprit is not the sin that is outside but the self that is inside.* Therein lies the problem. We're out of control, and we can't figure out what to do with ourselves.

Think about it this way. We have a filter. I call it the HAM filter—the "How about me?" filter. It is the device we use to judge everything, to see everything, to view life. It is a self-absorbed, self-centered, self-focused filter, and we look at the world through it. The decisions we make flow through the HAM filter—"How is this decision going to affect me?" So do the places we go—"What am I going to get out of it?" and the deals we make—"What's in it for me?" Everything in life flows through the HAM filter.

When we live with that kind of perspective, we make choices that have nothing to do with righteousness, nothing to do with reflecting the will of God or the image and character of God. The self-absorbed point of view has nothing to do with the life of holiness to which we're called. Instead, life is all about us. We try to make ourselves appear noble and sometimes even spiritual. Yet, we view life from the lens of the self—"How about me?" Is there any hope for freedom? Is there any way to change? Is it possible to conquer the *self.*

Perhaps you're wanting to cry out, "I don't want to be self-centered! I don't want to be self-focused! I don't want to be self-absorbed! I don't want to live for the self so that I am so easily entangled, entrapped, and ensnared in sin. How can I get past all that? How can I lose the HAM filter?" Paul said,

"I have been crucified with Christ and I no longer live, but Christ lives in me. The life I live in the body, I live by faith in the Son of God, who loved me and gave himself for me" (Gal. 2:20). Paul virtually shouts it out, "I have been crucified!" Crucifixion—Paul found it was the only way to real freedom. Crucifixion—it is the only way to conquer the self.

This book is about the power to conquer. But honestly, is there power in the Holy Spirit to truly conquer the self? Yes! But what about that word *crucify?* Can you actually crucify yourself? Let's go with that imagery for a moment. Imagine if someone laid a cross on the ground in front of you and gave you a hammer and three spikes and said, "Now crucify yourself." If from some reservoir of strength, you were able to pick up the hammer and bring yourself to nail your feet to the cross, if you stretched out your hand and were able to nail one hand to the wood, what about the hand that holds the hammer? Plus, how can you lift up yourself and the cross you're on? You couldn't do it! Physically impossible! We cannot nail ourselves to the cross spiritually any more than we can literally. We can't crucify ourselves. So what do we do?

We cry out, *Lord, here I am. Here is my* self. *I bring my* self *to You. I can't crucify my* self. *In fact, Lord, if You leave it up to me, I'm going to protect my* self. *I will lift up my* self. *I will advance my* self. *But I certainly can't crucify my* self. *Will You do it? Will You crucify me? Will You let me die to my* self *so that I can live for You?*

And then we hear the Word of God—*by the power of the*

*Holy Spirit* we can be more than conquerors, we can die to ourselves. Our *self* can be crucified! Victory over *self* is possible!

You may be wondering, "If I just pray and give myself fully to God, asking Him to crucify my *self* so that I am able to say that I have been crucified with Christ, will I ever have trouble with self again?" The answer is yes, you probably will —unless you do what Jesus says: "Take up [your] cross daily" (Luke 9:23). We must stay on the cross. They called for Jesus to come down from the Cross. They taunted Him by calling out, "Come down from the cross, if you are the Son of God!" (Matt. 27:40). They missed the whole point. The truth is, the reason Jesus didn't come down from the Cross was because He was who He said He was.

And as Christians we hear the world constantly calling us to come down from the cross. Like Jesus, we must answer no! If we are who we say we are, we must stay on the cross. As we do, the *self* is defeated and Christ gives us victory. We can conquer our *selves* only by the power of the Holy Spirit.

Aristotle said, "I count him braver who overcomes his desires than him who conquers his enemies. For the hardest victory is over self."[11]

# POWER TO CONQUER WORRY 9

**REMEMBER** Bobby McFerrin. He wrote the song
"Don't Worry, Be Happy." So what do you
think? Is the song right? Does the advice
work? Don't worry, be happy. It sounds
great when everything is going well,
doesn't it? It sounds wonderful and is so
easy to say, "Don't worry!"

Let's say life's going well for you.
Everything's fine. If someone comes up
and begins telling you about his or her
problems, what's the first thing you say?
"Don't worry about it. It's going to be OK."

But what if life isn't going so well
for you and you go to a friend and begin
telling him or her about your problems.
What does your friend say? "Don't worry
about it. It's going to be OK." But then

you respond, "Don't worry about it? What would you know? What are you talking about—don't worry about it?"

Have you ever had trouble with worry? I asked myself that question and thought, "No, I do it real well. Not a problem with me; I have no trouble worrying!" As you read this, are you thinking, *I'd like to learn from the Word of God about how to worry more—I'd like to spend more time in worry*? I doubt it.

There are many places in the Bible that tell us not to worry. Let's look at some excerpts from the Sermon on the Mount:

> Therefore, I tell you, do not worry about your life, what you will eat or drink; or about your body, what you will wear. Is not life more important than food, and the body more important than clothes? . . . Who of you by worrying can add a single hour to his life? And why do you worry about clothes? See how the lilies of the field grow. They do not labor or spin. . . . So do not worry, saying, "What shall we eat?" or "What shall we drink?" or "What shall we wear?" . . . Do not worry about tomorrow, for tomorrow will worry about itself. Each day has enough trouble of its own *(Matt. 6:25, 27-28, 31, 34)*.

Jesus was instructing His disciples privately about what to expect in their mission to the world. He warned them of the difficulties to come but told them, "When you are brought before synagogues, rulers and authorities, do not worry about how you will defend yourselves or what you will say" (Luke 12:11). Surely some of them were thinking, *You're kidding. Not worry about what we'll say?*

In Luke 10 we find the story of someone being consumed by worry. It is the story of Martha and Mary, the sisters of Lazarus, as Jesus was visiting at their home:

> As Jesus and his disciples were on their way, he came to a village where a woman named Martha opened her home to him. She had a sister called Mary, who sat at the Lord's feet listening to what he said. But Martha was distracted by all the preparations that had to be made. She came to him and asked, "Lord, don't you care that my sister has left me to do the work by myself? Tell her to help me!"
>
> "Martha, Martha," the Lord answered, "you are worried and upset about many things, but only one thing is needed. Mary has chosen what is better, and it will not be taken away from her" *(vv. 38-42)*.

I imagine that Martha had asked Mary to help. Maybe not directly, but using the signals that sisters use. And I imagine that Martha had finally had enough and figured, *I know how to get her to help me. I'll say something to Jesus.* So she spoke up: "Jesus, would You tell Mary to get up and help me? Doesn't it matter to You that she's making me do all the work? Don't You care?" And Jesus had an interesting response: "Martha, you are worried and upset."

I wonder if Martha gave the typical Christian response. You know what we usually do, don't you? We rename worry. "I'm not worried, Jesus. I'm just anxious and excited. I just have a lot to do to get the meal on the table. I'm just concerned." Jesus said, "You're worried." And maybe He looks at some of us today and says, "You're worried." And maybe as you consider this story, you're thinking, *I'm not really worried, Jesus. I'm just excited. I'm just anxious. There's just a lot to do, but I'm not worried.* Or maybe you're thinking, *Oh, no, what would I have to be worried about? I'm just losing my job!* Or, *I'm just waiting on a report from the doctor!* Or, *I'm just a parent with a child whose life is a mess! What do I have to worry about?* And Jesus says, "Don't

**"LIFE IS HARD."**

worry. Be happy." And we say, "Yeah, right. You're in heaven and we're here. Don't worry, be happy? You have no idea!"

So there's no doubt about it; we do worry and sometimes we worry a lot. But why do we worry? I thought about this as I was preparing this chapter and soon the answer just became so obvious. There are several reasons why we worry, and we don't have to dig too deep to find them. In fact, it didn't take long to put together this list of what I call Obvious Observations on Why We Worry.

The first is, "Life is hard." That's obvious, isn't it? It rains on the just and the unjust. Good things happen to bad people. Bad things happen to good people. And good and bad things happen to everybody in between. It's true; life is hard.

The second obvious reason we worry is, "The future is uncertain." We don't need to worry about tomorrow. Jesus even said, "Do not worry about tomorrow. . . . Each day has enough trouble of its own" (Matt. 6:34). That last part always bothered me: "Each day has enough trouble of its own." In other words, there are going to be plenty of things to bother you tomorrow—as if that's supposed to be encouraging.

The third obvious reason for worry is, "We're not in control." Now, some of us are more out of control than others. But in general, we're not in control of our lives. There's nothing we can do to control the future—but we can worry. And so we do.

Now at this point I could provide a list of all the reasons *not* to worry. But this has been done before and usually only causes frustration. I could also repeat some of the tried-but-true phrases that preachers have used for years to motivate and/or instill guilt in their hearers. For example, I could tell you that worrying about the future hampers your effectiveness today. Or that worrying does more harm than good. Or (this is a really good guilt inducer) that worry shows a lack of trust and faith in God.

I could list all those reasons that we're not supposed to worry, but I'm not going to give you that list because I don't want to frustrate you or leave you feeling guilty when you finish this chapter. Besides, the most compelling reason not to worry is because Jesus simply said, "Do not worry." Now that's pretty simple, isn't it? Just don't worry. But knowing we should not worry does not give us the *power* to overcome worry. I could say to you all day long, "Don't worry. Don't worry. Don't worry, be happy," and all that would come to your mind would be the things you're worrying about. Pretty counterproductive, don't you think?

Getting back to our story, we find Martha worrying.

143

Let's look closer at the language Luke uses here. There are four key words to examine. The first word is *distracted*. Look at what he says in verse 40: "But Martha was distracted by all of the preparations that had to be made." The Greek word translated *distracted* literally means "to drag around." This is the only place it's used in Scripture. Have you ever felt as if you were dragging around a whole lot of baggage? By baggage, I mean all of the mental and emotional clutter you drag around everywhere you go. It's the kind of clutter that preoccupies you when you're riding down the road and you're not thinking about the car that's about to run into you or the one you're about to run into. You're thinking about all this other stuff—you're *distracted*.

Look at the second word: *care*. It's the word Martha used when she addressed Jesus. "Lord, don't you *care?*" (emphasis added). The original means "to be of interest or concern." The idea basically stated is, "Doesn't it matter to You that I'm doing all this stuff by myself?" Have you ever wanted to ask God that question? "God, do You see where I am? Do You see the job that I'm doing? Do You see that I'm trying to be a good parent . . . a good spouse . . . a good son or daughter? That I'm trying to be a successful employee? God, don't You care? Does it matter to You at all what I'm doing?" You see, Martha had reached that place, that state of mind in those moments. "Lord, don't you care?"

And then Jesus used an interesting word: *worried*. He said, "Martha, Martha, . . . you are worried." The Greek word means "to be anxious about." It refers to an agitated state of mind. So the wheels in her mind were turning. Not only was she dragging all of this stuff around, not only did she feel as if Jesus didn't care, but she's also got this worried state of mind. She can't even get her mind settled on any one thing. It's going here and there; everything's got to get done.

And then the last word He uses is *upset*. He says, "You are worried and upset." *Upset* comes from the word that means "to be disturbed." In fact, in Greek, the word actually is transliterated into *turbid* or *turbulence*. Have you ever been on a plane when the pilot announces, "We're about to experience some turbulence in the area, so we'd like you to fasten your seat belts." And just as your seat belt's fastened, you hear the plane go *Whooooom!* and it just drops. And your stomach is somewhere above you in the overhead storage bin. You feel as if you need to reach up to find your stomach and your heart up above those oxygen masks.

That's the sort of thing that was going on inside of Martha. So she blurted out, "Lord, don't you care?" And Jesus responds (paraphrased), "You're worried and upset over *many* things going through your mind and emotions. But there is only one thing that is necessary. It's not the roast. It's not the beans burning. It's not any of those things. You're worried about many things, but there's only one thing that's of primary importance right here, and Mary has chosen it. And I am not going to make her get up and worry with you. I'm not going to say, 'Mary, Martha's pretty much going crazy right now, so just get up and help her and then we'll come back to what we're talking about here.' No, I'm not going to

145

do that because what Mary has chosen is *better*" (the word actually means "good"). He wasn't saying that what Martha was doing was *bad* but just that Mary's choice was *better.* Mary wasn't worried; Martha was. And Jesus was chastising Martha for her worry.

Have you ever been gently chastised by the Holy Spirit for worry? Have you heard the Holy Spirit, the still small voice, say, "You shouldn't worry about this situation. Let Me take care of it"? And yet we say, "Right. Yeah. You're in heaven; I'm here. How are we going to do this?"

So is there really power to conquer worry? Is it possible to stop the worry in our lives? Perhaps the first step toward ending worry is recognizing that worry does not accomplish anything worthwhile. Not only does worry not help, but it often has the opposite effect. Worried about losing your hair? Worrying about it may speed up the process! Worried about losing your health? The adverse effects of worry may actually cause detrimental effects on your health; it certainly won't make you healthier. Worried about losing your job? That could actually cause poor job performance and become a self-fulfilling prophecy. Worried about gaining weight? You may wind up eating more to deal with your worry. The writer of Proverbs says, "An anxious heart weighs a man down" (Prov. 12:25). Another wise person once wrote, "Worry is like a rocking chair; it gives you something to do, but it doesn't get you anywhere." Worry doesn't accomplish anything.

There's the story of a man who was out driving one night on a dark, country road and he had a flat tire. So he got out, opened his trunk, and discovered that his jack was missing. Looking around to see if there was any place where he could get help, he saw a porch light shining in the distance. So he walked down the dark, country road to the porch light, which was at a farmer's house. As he was walking, he began to think, *I wonder if that man's had people try to break in and steal his chickens or his cows or something like that? He probably has a shotgun he keeps right above the door. And I bet he's probably got a couple of pit bulls out in the front yard, and as soon as I get there, he's going to turn those pit bulls loose on me and he's going to grab that shotgun, and he's going to pepper me as I'm running away in the distance.* The man finally reached the house and banged on the door. The farmer came to the door, wiped the sleep out of his eyes, and was taken aback when the man yelled, "I didn't want your old jack anyway!"

Isn't that what we do? We get all worked up and we assume the worst. And everything we thought was going to be bad turns out fine. All of our assumptions were wrong. But we worry. So we can agree that worry does not accomplish anything. But does that help us conquer worry? Not really. Knowing in my head that worry doesn't accomplish anything doesn't stop me from worrying, because there's more to it than that.

Maybe the way to overcome worry is to realize that God loves us. It's true: God loves you. That's the greatest truth you will ever hear, probably the most simple, but definitely the greatest. *God loves you.* Listen to the compassion in Jesus' voice: "Martha, Martha." I don't hear frustration here. Maybe there is. Maybe I'm just reading too much into this. But I don't think Jesus is frustrated with Martha. I think He's saying, "Martha, listen to Me. You need to stop this. You're worried, upset. You need to stop. Come in here and sit down."

In 12:22-26 Luke deals with worry in a little more detail when he records Jesus' words to His disciples: "Therefore I tell you, do not worry about your life, what you will eat; or about your body, what you will wear. Life is more than food, and the body more than clothes. Consider the ravens: They do not sow or reap, they have no storeroom or barn; yet God feeds them." Now here's the clincher: "And how much more valuable you are than [birds]!" He wasn't devaluing birds; God takes care of the birds. Jesus is saying, "How much more valuable are you than they! Who of you by worrying can add a single hour to his life? Since you cannot do this very little thing, why do you worry?" Now, would you consider extending the length of your life "a very little thing"? I sure wouldn't, but to God it is a little thing. You see, the One who created eternity says:

> Since you cannot do this very *little* thing, why do you worry about the rest? Consider how the lilies grow. They do not labor or spin, but I tell you not even Solomon in all his splendor was dressed like one of these. If that is how God clothes the grass of the field, which is here today and tomorrow is thrown into the fire, how much more will he clothe you, O you of little faith! And do not set your heart on what you will eat or drink; do

not worry about it. For the pagan world runs after all such things, and your Father knows that you need them. But seek his kingdom, and these things will be given to you as well *(vv. 26-31, emphasis added).*

You see, that entire passage takes it a little further, explains a little more about the emotion Jesus is feeling when He says (paraphrased), "Martha, Martha, you're worried. You're upset. That doesn't need to happen. Mary has chosen what is good. She's chosen the better. I'm not going to take that away from her."

Yes, if we want to stop worrying, we have to understand that God loves us. He gets involved in the stuff of our lives. He gets His hands dirty with the things that just rock our world and send us into all kinds of turbulence. Our lives are not some divine *Survivor* show where God is sitting back and saying, "Well, let's see who's going to get voted off this week, and let's see who's going to get immunity." That is *not* what God does. He gets *involved.* If He feeds the birds and you're more important than the birds, if He takes care of the grasses of the fields that are here today and thrown into the fire tomorrow, how much more . . . you see?

So you know that God loves you, and you know that worry doesn't help you accomplish anything, but does that help you to conquer worry? A little bit, but not entirely.

The real answer to worry is found in Mary's role in the story. Look at her actions. Notice two things: where she was and what she was doing. Where was Mary? She was sitting at the Lord's feet. Where do we need to be? At the feet of God.

149

Worry is conquered when we are sitting at the Lord's feet, when we are in proximity to Jesus, when we are in His presence. Mary was in a position of submission. She had submitted all of her stuff to God.

Look at what Mary was doing: she was listening to what Jesus was saying. The word that is used here for *listening* means "continual listening." She wasn't just catching a word every now and then. She wasn't looking at Martha or thinking about what Martha was doing. She wasn't thinking about all of the preparation that needed to be made. Instead, she was continually listening to Jesus. She was hanging on His every word. She was in essence directing her mind and attention to Christ. No wonder she wasn't worried! We have the power to conquer worry if we live in this awareness of the presence of God in our lives and if we just trust Him enough to take Him at His word, to hear His word and to apply it to our lives.

How can we conquer worry? Well, look at what had seized the attention of the women in our story. Mary was occupied with Jesus and she was blessed. Martha was occupied with her situation and she was stressed. Maybe it has something to do with where we are and what we're looking at or listening to. Maybe it has something to do with where we focus our attention.

Can we really have the power to conquer worry? Yes, we can. We have to confess our worry to God, to name it. We can't mask it or pretend it's something different by saying, "Well, I'm just nervous, anxious, excited, or a little distracted." No. We need to call it what it is.

Hear the words of Jesus: "You're worried and upset."

Admit it. "OK, Lord, You're right. I'm worried. And the only way to deal with this is to focus my attention on You. I'm going to submit to You the things that are causing me to worry. I'm going to take them and place them right at Your feet. And I'm going to sit here at Your feet in submission and listen to what You have to say to me. Every word, I'm going to hear it." And the Holy Spirit will begin to speak. You'll begin to get into the Word of God, and you'll hear what the Lord has to say to you. And somehow, someway, in a divine moment, in a divine way, the Holy Spirit will take His Word and do something in your life to empower you to overcome worry in your situation. But, again, that power comes when we put ourselves at the feet of Jesus and focus our attention on *who* He is.

We have to stop asking "What if?" and start asking "Who is?" *"What if* this happens?" Stop asking that question. Stop it. Quit it. *"Who is* with me? *Who is* in control?" Those are the questions to ask.

What's ironic to me is that Martha says, "Don't you care?" And the fact is, Jesus cared more than Martha even realized. In fact, He cared more about what was best for her and for that situation than she did. Sometimes when I look at the situations in my life that cause me to worry, I want to say, "Lord, don't You care?" Yet, I have to stop and remember, "Lord, You care even more than I care. You care more about my children than I do. You care more about my job than I do. You care about my life more than I do. And if You care, and if You love me, then I know You're going to take care of all these things."

151

If you're dealing with worry in your life, there's a better way to deal with it than just saying, "I'm just going to pick myself up by my own bootstraps and conquer this worry. I'm just not going to worry anymore." That doesn't work; you've probably already tried it many times. There's a better way. Sit at His feet. Listen to His words. Trust Jesus enough to focus your attention on Him. And you'll begin to get a new glimpse of His power, His purity, His love, His grace, and His mercy with which He just wants to envelop you. And all of those things that cause you to worry will be put into their proper place.

I won't be naive or ignorant and tell you that all of your problems will be solved the way you want them to be. No, some problems don't go away that easily. Some problems are not solvable right away. Some problems, some issues, we have to learn to live with and cope with. But there is a power, a strength that moves us beyond our own resources, that enables us to trust God. Come before the Lord and sit at His feet and say, "Here are the things that I've been worrying about, Lord. I'm going to put them right here before You, and I want Your Spirit to do Your work in me to help me release these things. Free me from worry, Lord, so that I may begin to sing a new song of trust, a song of joy, a song of peace."

# POWER TO CONQUER TRAGEDY

## 10

**A DRUNK** driver crosses the line, hits a car, and kills a family, a mom or a dad, a brother or a sister. How does a person deal with a tragedy like that?

A man who has lived for Christ all of his life and has taken good care of himself contracts terminal cancer. No real explanation is offered. No answers given. How do we cope with such a horrible loss?

Consider the child who is a victim of abuse or the child who is born with disease or contracts a deadly illness early on. How do we deal with such heartbreak? And where in the world is God in all of this?

People believe a lot of things when tragedy occurs. Some believe that tragedy is simply fate—"what will be, will be." Everything is predetermined. If we believe this, we can just curse fate and accept what has happened as if we are simply victims.

People who believe in fate may react differently to tragedy. Some choose to express their emotions and really experience the heart-wrenching impact of tragedy. Others are more stoic and say, "I'm not going to suffer," and they build walls around their senses and emotions to avoid feeling anything. But either way, these people accept their circumstances as a matter of fate.

The problem with this view is that not all tragedy can be simply blamed on fate. There is usually a cause for every effect. It seems to me that unless *everything* can be accredited to fate, then fate loses its credibility. There are some events we cannot accredit to fate. Some consequences are obviously the result of choice.

Early in my first pastorate, one of the funerals I had to preach was especially difficult. A 20-year-old young man, Jimmy, was killed in a motorcycle accident. You might ask, "Was that fate? Was that choice? Which was it?" Jimmy was high on drugs. He stole the motorcycle, was running from the police, and hit a palm tree head-on.

Tragic? Yes. Fate? No! The accident was a result of choice. That may sound cold; it may sound hard. But it was choice—a choice that Jimmy made.

A second common belief that people have is that tragedy is Satan's fault. Comedian Flip Wilson starred in his own variety show in the early 1970s, and he made people laugh every week when his Geraldine character declared, "The devil made me do it!" It was a great punch line, but some people blame every tragic situation on Satan.

Views on Satan's influence and existence range between two extremes. At one extreme is the opinion that Satan does not exist, that there is no literal devil. The Christian version of this idea is that Satan entered into Judeo-Christian thought through Persian Zoroastrianism, which teaches that a god of good and a god of evil are in a continual battle with each other—a battle whose outcome is unknown. This was the religion of the Babylonians when Israel was in exile. Some believe the idea of a personified devil or a literal Satan entered into Judeo-Christian thought at that time.

At the other extreme is the belief that Satan is to blame for every tragedy, that a demon or a devil is at work behind everything bad that happens.

I firmly believe that Jesus would not let us believe a lie. He always taught the truth. And He taught the existence of a literal Satan. But even with that, He did not blame everything on the devil. As a matter of fact, in one of the clearest passages about how sin gets into our lives, James writes that after we are tempted through our own evil desires, we join our will to those desires, and then our sin, when it is full grown, produces death (see James 1:13-15). Satan is not even mentioned. So we can't blame every bad thing on Satan. He will be found guilty ultimately, but he's not the scapegoat for all of our choices.

There is a third set of common beliefs that are about God. The beliefs range from denying the existence of God to asserting that His influence is limited in some way. Some people argue, "If God is all-good, and God is all-powerful, then why is there evil in the world?" Good question. The answer that follows usually is, "Because if God is all-good, then He must not be all-powerful, because He would surely drive out all evil—but that doesn't happen, so He must not be able to do it." Or "If God is all-powerful, then He could drive out all evil—but He doesn't, so He must not be all-good." Related to this is a view called deism, whose adherents say, "We want to believe there is a God, so God must have wound up the universe, like some big clock, and set it in motion, and then stepped back and let it go. He doesn't involve himself in the affairs of the world anymore." Then there are agnostics, who say, "There is a God, but we cannot know anything about Him." This view doesn't add up. How can you believe God exists if you can't know Him and He refuses to reveal himself?

The problem with all of these viewpoints is that life—all of life, whether or not you're a Christian—is based on faith. We live on the foundation of faith—faith that there is a God; faith that there is no God; faith that we cannot know God; faith that God just wound the world up and put it in motion. What we have to do is decide where we're going to put our faith.

Where we place our faith affects our outlook and how we relate to others. For example, if we believe there is no God, then we have no hope for the future or the present, and there is no healing from the past. And this simply does not satisfy our minds and hearts. Try comforting someone who is facing tragedy by saying, "Well, there is no God. So anyway . . ." See how much comfort they get from that. See how much sense is made of life in those moments. It just won't satisfy. It won't cut it.

Another commonly held belief is that God is punishing us. A lot of Christians suffer from this negative view. "The tragedy in my life is a result from earlier sin. God is punishing me for what I did in the past."

## ISN'T GOD A GRACIOUS GOD?

When I was a child, I knew a woman who had a daughter born with both Down syndrome and a hole in her heart. A group of the woman's friends gathered around and told her the reason that her baby was born that way and that God did not heal her child was because she had unconfessed sin in her life. Now this dear lady was a very strong Christian and was deeply involved in ministry. Yet people still had the nerve to say, "Oh, there's unconfessed sin in your life. That's why God refuses to heal your baby."

Satan uses this argument to attack a lot of believers. Now it's true that we all have a past. Even the Scriptures say, "All have sinned and fall short of the glory of God" (Rom. 3:23). But if God is punishing us for our sins from the past—even though we are believers now, even though we have accepted Him—what happened to the sacrifice of Jesus Christ?

It's also true that no believer is flawless. There are areas of our lives still needing the transforming work of God. But are we to interpret the tragedy in our lives as a consequence of our flaws?

What happened to the whole concept of grace? Isn't God a gracious God? Doesn't He cast our sins into the "sea of forgetfulness" never to be remembered against us anymore? Are not all the wrong acts we've committed gone? Past? Over? Finished? And are we not now new creatures before Christ Jesus? Does God's grace not continue transforming us today?

Satan wants to remind us of our past sins—the sins of our youth, of our teen years. He wants to defeat us by saying God is punishing us for our past. He wants us to believe that we get what we deserve and that our flaws are the cause of our tragedies. But when he tries to do this, we need to remind ourselves that we are saved by God's grace and that through Jesus Christ God has forgiven our past. We truly have been made new again and are being transformed into His image.

A fifth common belief about tragedy asserts that God caused it. It came from Him, and He knows best. It is for a greater good. Have you ever heard that? That just doesn't make sense. Are people who accept this view saying the reason your child died was that God knows best and it's part of His plan? The reason the family was tragically killed was that God knows best and He did it? That just doesn't hold water. In the early 20th century, 6 million Jews were tortured to death; for what greater good was that? And what about September 11? All I have to do is say the date. Twenty-seven hundred people who were minding their own business, people with families, people with children, people with parents—all of a sudden they are dying because a group of people hates the United States—and that's supposed to be for a greater good? God did that? *Absolutely not!*

God would not sacrifice one soul, not one life—other than His own—for a greater good of saving someone else. I can't believe that He would. It's simply not in keeping with His character. It's not in line with His nature. That would be a different sort of god from the one portrayed in Scripture. The only life God calls for in sacrifice to save another life is His own, and He gave it.

There's still another common belief concerning tragedy: God permits tragedy, but He doesn't plan it or cause it. For most people, this is a way of dealing with the permissive will of God. For most people, this refers to a specific incident. So when my cousin, who was a very careful driver in his latter teenage years, was making a right-hand turn in a 35 miles-per-hour zone, and a drunk driver was coming over the top of that hill at over 100 miles per hour and hit his car and killed him—you're telling me God just *allowed* that to happen? Where is the comfort in that? Where is the peace? What is the difference between God *allowing* it and God *causing* it? There is no practical difference. I don't believe this is consistent with the character of God either. There are a lot of arguments against this thought, but this is my biggest problem with it: There is no practical difference between God allowing it and God causing it. The deed is done. The heart is broken. Tragedy has occurred.

Some folks say, "God *allowed* it to happen in order to get a greater good out of it." We've already looked at that argument. I don't buy it. It says God would be telling a parent, "I'm not going to take your child away from you, but I'm going to *allow* it to be done. I'm going to let your child die so a greater purpose can be accomplished." That's a copout; it's an attempt to make excuses for God.

*So, how do we conquer tragedy?* The clue is in understanding the source of tragedy *and* who God is—what we believe about God. So let's look at that first part: Where does tragedy come from?

First of all, we know that some tragedies come from human choices. Did you smoke all your life? You're a candidate for lung cancer. Do you get behind the wheel of a car after having too much alcohol to drink? You're likely to have a car accident. Is that God's fault? Did God "allow" it for some purpose? *No!* It's a result of human choice. So there are some tragedies that are caused directly from human choices.

But tragedy is rooted in something deeper than human choice. Tragedy comes from living in a world that is permeated with sin. That's not to say that every time there's a tragedy in our lives, it is the result of our own sin; but rather, a sin-permeated world will produce tragedy.

Our theology works like this: We believe God is love. He is holy love, and holy love calls for a freedom of choice. Love grants us a choice—a grace-empowered choice.

Some people say we don't have a choice because that would hurt the sovereignty of God. Let me tell you: God *is* sovereign. He chooses to limit himself, and He gives us a choice. That does not in any way reflect any weakness in God; it is His strength. He could have taken away our choice if He so desired, because He is God; He is sovereign. But instead, He chose to create us in His image and enter into a love relationship with us, which means that you and I were granted a choice. In the scheme of life, we humans took the gift of choice and abused it. We abused our freedom and chose to sin against God. Therefore, as Paul states, "Sin entered the world through one man, and death through sin" (Rom. 5:12). As a result of the sin of Adam and Eve, we live in a sin-permeated world and there are tragedies that happen solely because we are in this world.

Now what does God do? I guess God could say, "Well, I'll just intervene in the world and I'll make all the wrong all right one day. There'll be no more sin, and there'll be no more tragedy. How does that sound to you?" Sounds like heaven. Sounds like something He has already set in motion, doesn't it? But in the meantime, we live in a world that is dominated by sin, and when we live in this world, we have to endure tragedy.

So where is God in all of this? Where on earth is God? In Rom. 8:35 Paul writes: "Who shall separate us from the love of Christ? Shall trouble or hardship or persecution or famine or nakedness or danger or sword?" He's referring here to the multiple ways that tragedy can strike our lives. He continues:

As it is written: "For your sake we face death all day long; we are considered as sheep to be slaughtered." No, in all these things we are more than conquerors through him who loved us. For I am convinced that neither death nor life, neither angels nor demons, neither the present nor the future, nor any powers, neither height nor depth, nor anything else in all creation, will be able to separate us from the love of God that is in Christ Jesus our Lord *(vv. 36-39).*

So where on earth is God in all of this? Let me tell you: God is walking with us, weeping with us, and suffering with us. God is with us and God is for us. If you

**GOD IS WALKING WITH US.**

look around in the midst of tragedy and you want to know where God is, He is right there closer than a brother. He has not forsaken you, and He is not punishing you. He is there with you. Satan has not gotten the upper hand on Him. As we live out our lives in this sin-dominated world, God is with us. So what is He doing? Is He just there or is He doing something too? Well, if He's just there, I guarantee that's enough, but He is also doing something. Look at Rom. 8:26-27: "In the same way, the Spirit helps us in our weakness. We do not know what we ought to pray for, but the Spirit himself intercedes for us with groans that words cannot express. And he who searches our hearts knows the mind of the Spirit, because the Spirit intercedes for the saints in accordance with God's will." The Holy Spirit is praying for us.

I want you to notice how close the Spirit is to us. We know what we *ought* to say, but He knows what *needs* to be said. We often don't even know what the will of God is, but He knows the will of God. And so the Holy Spirit does for us what we can't even do for ourselves. He is so close that He knows our heart. He knows how it's breaking. He knows what tragedy has done to us, and out of that He is praying for us in accordance with the will of God. And there's no better place to be than the will of God.

Take note of verse 28, a very familiar passage of Scripture: "And we know that in all things God works for the good of those who love him, who have been called according to his purpose." So, "in all things God *works*," and from the Greek word here we get the English word *synergy*. In other words, God takes the junk of life, all the tragedies, all the problems, all Paul listed in verse 35—the troubles, hardships, persecution, famine, nakedness, danger, sword, and so forth—and He in effect says: "This comes from living in a sin-permeated world, but I'm not going to let it have the last word. In fact, I'm going to take it and I'm going to pull it all together. I'm going to synergize it, and out of it something good is going to happen. It's going to be redeemed." The mother's heart that's broken, the friend's heart that's pierced, God is going to redeem all of it. The abuse that occurred early in life to an innocent victim, God is going to redeem that too. He's going to take all that stuff, all the tragedy, and work it together and bring out of it something good.

Listen to the word *good*. What did Jesus say about the

word *good?* He said there is only One who is good—*God* (see Matt. 19:17). In other words, God's going to take the junk in our lives and work something godly out of it. That's what He does for us. And only God can do that.

You see, if you do not have God, you do not have hope. The best thing we can offer to someone going through tragedy is a hug, to hold him or her and say, "I'll pray for you." But that's it. But if the person will turn his or her heart toward God, He'll take the tragedy and work something good.

Now notice what Paul says in Rom. 8:29: "For those God foreknew he also predestined to be conformed to the likeness of his Son, that he might be called the firstborn among many brothers." The word *predestined* is a word most Wesleyans like to avoid. But let me tell you what that word means. It does not mean "to limit"; it means "to choose." Now put that in the context of Scripture to see what Paul's really talking about here. Here's what he's saying: "God has chosen us." Chosen who? Chosen a few for heaven and others for hell? No. God has chosen *all* of humanity to be the objects of His love. God has chosen *all* of humanity to be the objects of His grace. There is no one who stands outside of the choice of God. And God has justified those of us who have accepted our chosenness, those of us who have listened to His voice. He has dealt with the sins of the past, and those whom He justified, He glorified.

We often think of *glorified* in terms of what happens when we die, but glory involves the image and presence of God. In other words, God puts His image in us and His presence with us. Again, He is with us; He is for us. And He takes all of the junk and He works it for our good.

Consider again the word of the Lord: "What, then, shall we say in response to this? If God is for us, who can be against us?" (v. 31). *God is for us.* That makes all the difference. "He who did not spare his own Son, but gave him up for us all—how will he not also, along with him, graciously give us all things?" (v. 32). This demonstrates how much God is for us: He laid down His very life.

When you're going through tragedy and you wonder where on earth God is, He is with you. What is He doing? He's praying for you. He's working all of these circumstances together to make something good in your life and to redeem the tragedy so that it is not without ultimate value.

Let's look again at Paul's words: "Who will bring any charge against those whom God has chosen? It is God who justifies. Who is he that condemns? Christ Jesus, who died—more than that, who was raised to life—is at the right hand of God and is also interceding for us" (vv. 33-34). We have the Holy Spirit praying for us. We have the Father working all things together. And we have the Son at the right hand of the Father interceding for us. We have all the members of the Trinity bringing all of their resources to bear on our circumstances.

Our God cares when our hearts are broken. Our God cares when we face tragedy. And our God says: "I'm not going to let that tragedy have the last word. I'm going to pull it together. I'm going to make it good. I'm going to make it right."

In the midst of it all, God is for us. God is with us.

In the midst of the tragedy, God is for us. God is with us.

In the midst of adversity, God is for us. God is with us.

In the midst of pain, God is for us. God is with us.

In the midst of heartache, God is for us. God is with us.

In the midst of questions, God is for us. God is with us.

In the midst of disappointment and evil, God is for us. God is with us.

So, how do we conquer tragedy? Romans 8:37 says: "In all these things, we are more than conquerors." You know what the word *conqueror* means? It means, well, *conqueror.* Think about what a conqueror is. A conqueror has enemies to defeat, obstacles to overcome, and situations to face and win over.

*We* are more than conquerors. This is not just a self-help thing. "We are more than conquerors"—and don't leave off the last part—"through him who loved us." Through His love, through Christ and all of His love, we can conquer tragedy!

If you have faced tragedy in your life—maybe it was 20 years ago, maybe it was 20 minutes ago, maybe you're in the middle of it right now—and you wonder, "How am I going to deal with this?" The answer is, only through Jesus Christ.

What is the source of tragedy? We live in a sin-permeated world and tragedy is going to happen, but God will change that one day. We call it heaven. We're going to live in His presence forever, in a peace-filled kingdom where tragedy is no more.

But what do we believe about God? We believe He is

with us. In the midst of tragedy, we can look for the hand of God, and when we ask, "God, where are You?" we can know, "You're praying for me. You're interceding for me. You're taking this event and this circumstance and this tragedy, and You're working it all together. And somehow God, You're going to redeem it in an incredible way."

When all is said and done, there is no totally satisfying explanation for tragedy. All we can say is that we live in a sin-filled world. But we do know this one thing: *God is with us.*

# THE POWER SOURCE 11

MY wife, Karan, and I have recently experienced the joy of constructing a house. Now, if you've never built a house together, you're in for a treat. There are few things that can try a relationship like building a house. In fact, we were told at the beginning of the process that if our marriage can survive the construction of a house, then it is a solid marriage. Before you worry about us, let me assure you that we're fine. We did even better than survive!

A house goes through various stages as it is being constructed. At one point the house looked complete. The water was working, the transformer box was installed, the outside was finished, the trim was in place, the walls were

171

painted, flooring was down, the lights were hung, and even the light bulbs were in the sockets. If you walked into the house during the daylight, it looked great. But when the nighttime came and the darkness engulfed the house, all you could see was nothing—total darkness.

I discovered a major problem. Even though everything was in place, no one had taken the time to contact the electric company so the power could be connected to the house. The power source was there. The house was ready and in desperate need of power. But there was no connection to the power source. The house had not been *plugged* in. It looked complete but was not functional. After all of the work, all of the time, all of the money, all of the effort, all of the worry, and all of the pain (I broke a toe and hit a few fingers with the hammer), I was still left sitting in the darkness.

How often are we guilty of this approach to life? We work and we worry. We invest incredible amounts of time and money. We experience all of the pain. We even have a product that looks complete. Yet, it is not functional in everyday life. And we still sit in the darkness.

Could it be we are not connected to the right power source? Could our problem be that we're not plugged in to the source of great power? Perhaps so.

Once again I mention the words of Paul in Rom. 8:37: "In all these things we are more than conquerors *through him* who loved us" (emphasis added). In order for us to be more than conquerors in all of life, we must be connected to the power source—the true source of real power.

It is through our *continual* connection to the true power source in Christ Jesus that we will be made more than victorious. There is no other source of real power. You can't save yourself. There are some problems you just can't fix and some obstacles you just can't overcome. But *through Him*, through real power, divine power, creative power, we can overcome.

Power is a valuable commodity. It always has been and always will be. We desperately need it. And it is available. Like the situation at our house, the source is virtually sitting on your doorstep. Plug in. Connect. You can have the power to conquer.

# EPILOGUE

## Power Connections

Paul wrote to Timothy, "All scripture is God-breathed and is useful for teaching, rebuking, correcting and training in righteousness" (2 Tim. 3:16). The epilogue is filled with "God-breathed" scriptures that will connect you to the source of real power—God's power.

### Exod. 15:6

Your right hand, O LORD, was majestic in power. Your right hand, O LORD, shattered the enemy.

### 1 Chron. 29:11

Yours, O LORD, is the greatness and the power and the glory and the majesty and the splendor, for everything in heaven and earth is yours. Yours, O LORD, is the kingdom; you are exalted as head over all.

### 1 Chron. 29:12

Wealth and honor come from you; you are the ruler of all things. In your hands are strength and power to exalt and give strength to all.

### 2 Chron. 20:6

O LORD, God of our fathers, are you not the God who is in heaven? You rule over all the kingdoms of the nations. Power and might are in your hand, and no one can withstand you.

## 2 Chron. 20:12

O our God, will you not judge them? For we have no power to face this vast army that is attacking us. We do not know what to do, but our eyes are upon you.

## Job 12:13

To God belong wisdom and power; counsel and understanding are his.

## Ps. 20:6

Now I know that the LORD saves his anointed; he answers him from his holy heaven with the saving power of his right hand.

## Ps. 63:2

I have seen you in the sanctuary and beheld your power and your glory.

## Ps. 66:3

Say to God, "How awesome are your deeds! So great is your power that your enemies cringe before you."

## Ps. 66:7

He rules forever by his power, his eyes watch the nations—let not the rebellious rise up against him. Selah

## Ps. 68:28

Summon your power, O God; show us your strength, O God, as you have done before.

## Ps. 68:34

Proclaim the power of God, whose majesty is over Israel, whose power is in the skies.

## Ps. 68:35

You are awesome, O God, in your sanctuary; the God of Israel gives power and strength to his people. Praise be to God!

## Ps. 71:18

Even when I am old and gray, do not forsake me, O God, till I declare your power to the next generation, your might to all who are to come.

## Ps. 77:14

You are the God who performs miracles; you display your power among the peoples.

## Ps. 78:4

We will tell the next generation the praiseworthy deeds of the LORD, his power, and the wonders he has done.

## Ps. 89:13

Your arm is endued with power; your hand is strong, your right hand exalted.

## Ps. 145:6

They will tell of the power of your awesome works, and I will proclaim your great deeds.

## Ps. 147:5

Great is our Lord and mighty in power; his understanding has no limit.

## Ps. 150:2

Praise him for his acts of power; praise him for his surpassing greatness.

## Isa. 33:13

You who are far away, hear what I have done; you who are near, acknowledge my power!

## Isa. 40:10

See, the Sovereign LORD comes with power, and his arm rules for him. See, his reward is with him, and his recompense accompanies him.

## Isa. 40:26-31

Lift your eyes and look to the heavens: Who created all these? He who brings out the starry host one by one, and calls them each by name. Because of his great power and mighty strength, not one of them is missing. Why do you say, O Jacob, and complain, O Israel, "My way is hidden from the LORD; my cause is disregarded by my God"? Do you not know? Have you not heard? The LORD is the everlasting God, the Creator of the ends of the earth. He will not grow tired or weary, and his understanding no one can fathom. He gives strength to the weary and increases the power of the weak. Even youths grow tired and weary, and young men stumble and fall; but those who hope in the LORD will renew their strength. They will soar on wings like eagles; they will run and not grow weary, they will walk and not be faint.

## Jer. 10:6

No one is like you, O LORD; you are great, and your name is mighty in power.

## Jer. 10:12

But God made the earth by his power; he founded the world by his wisdom and stretched out the heavens by his understanding.

## Jer. 16:21

Therefore I will teach them—this time I will teach them my power and might. Then they will know that my name is the LORD.

## Jer. 27:5

With my great power and outstretched arm I made the earth and its people and the animals that are on it, and I give it to anyone I please.

## Jer. 32:17

Ah, Sovereign LORD, you have made the heavens and the earth by your great power and outstretched arm. Nothing is too hard for you.

## Jer. 51:15

He made the earth by his power; he founded the world by his wisdom and stretched out the heavens by his understanding.

## Dan. 2:20

Praise be to the name of God for ever and ever; wisdom and power are his.

## Dan. 7:14

He was given authority, glory and sovereign power; all peoples, nations and men of every language worshiped him. His dominion is an everlasting dominion that will not pass away, and his kingdom is one that will never be destroyed.

## Zech. 4:6

"Not by might nor by power, but by my Spirit," says the Lord Almighty.

## Luke 4:36

All the people were amazed and said to each other, "What is this teaching? With authority and power he gives orders to evil spirits and they come out!"

## Luke 6:19

And the people all tried to touch him, because power was coming from him and healing them all.

## Luke 9:1

When Jesus had called the Twelve together, he gave them power and authority to drive out all demons and to cure diseases.

## Luke 24:49

I am going to send you what my Father has promised; but stay in the city until you have been clothed with power from on high.

## John 17:11

I will remain in the world no longer, but they are still in the world, and I am coming to you. Holy Father, protect them by the power of your name—the name you gave me—so that they may be one as we are one.

## Acts 1:8

But you will receive power when the Holy Spirit comes on you; and you will be my witnesses in Jerusalem, and in all Judea and Samaria, and to the ends of the earth.

## Acts 4:33

With great power the apostles continued to testify to the resurrection of the Lord Jesus, and much grace was upon them all.

## Acts 6:8

Now Stephen, a man full of God's grace and power, did great wonders and miraculous signs among the people.

## Rom. 1:16

I am not ashamed of the gospel, because it is the power of God for the salvation of everyone who believes: first for the Jew, then for the Gentile.

## Rom. 4:21

[Abraham was] fully persuaded that God had power to do what he had promised.

## Rom. 15:13

May the God of hope fill you with all joy and peace as you trust in him, so that you may overflow with hope by the power of the Holy Spirit.

## 1 Cor. 1:18

For the message of the cross is foolishness to those who are perishing, but to us who are being saved it is the power of God.

## 1 Cor. 1:23-24

We preach Christ crucified: a stumbling block to Jews and foolishness to Gentiles, but to those whom God has called, both Jews and Greeks, Christ the power of God and the wisdom of God.

## 1 Cor. 2:4-5

My message and my preaching were not with wise and persuasive words, but with a demonstration of the Spirit's power, so that your faith might not rest on men's wisdom, but on God's power.

## 1 Cor. 4:20

For the kingdom of God is not a matter of talk but of power.

## 1 Cor. 6:14

By his power God raised the Lord from the dead, and he will raise us also.

## 2 Cor. 4:7

But we have this treasure in jars of clay to show that this all-surpassing power is from God and not from us.

## 2 Cor. 10:4

The weapons we fight with are not the weapons of the world. On the contrary, they have divine power to demolish strongholds.

## 2 Cor. 12:9

"My grace is sufficient for you, for my power is made perfect in weakness." Therefore I will boast all the more gladly about my weaknesses, so that Christ's power may rest on me.

## Eph. 3:16-21

I pray that out of his glorious riches he may strengthen you with power through his Spirit in your inner being, so that Christ may dwell in your hearts through faith. And I pray that you, being rooted and established in love, may have power, together with all the saints, to grasp how wide and long and high and deep is the love of Christ, and to know this love that surpasses knowledge—that you may be filled to the measure of all the fullness of God. Now to him who is able to do immeasurably more than all we ask or imagine, according to his power that is at work within us, to him be glory in the church and in Christ Jesus throughout all generations, for ever and ever! Amen.

## Eph. 6:10

Finally, be strong in the Lord and in his mighty power.

## Phil. 3:10-11

I want to know Christ and the power of his resurrection and the fellowship of sharing in his sufferings, becoming like him in his death, and so, somehow, to attain to the resurrection from the dead.

## Phil. 3:21

Who [Jesus Christ], by the power that enables him to bring everything under his control, will transform our lowly bodies so that they will be like his glorious body.

## Col. 1:10-14

And we pray this in order that you may live a life worthy of the Lord and may please him in every way: bearing fruit in every good work, growing in the knowledge of God, being strengthened with all power according to his glorious might so that you may have great endurance and patience, and joyfully giving thanks to the Father, who has qualified you to share in the inheritance of the saints in the kingdom of light. For he has rescued us from the dominion of darkness and brought us into the kingdom of the Son he loves, in whom we have redemption, the forgiveness of sins.

## 2 Thess. 1:11

With this in mind, we constantly pray for you, that our God may count you worthy of his calling, and that by his power he may fulfill every good purpose of yours and every act prompted by your faith.

## 2 Tim. 1:7-9

For God did not give us a spirit of timidity, but a spirit of power, of love and of self-discipline. So do not be ashamed to testify about our Lord, or ashamed of me his prisoner. But join with me in suffering for the gospel, by the power of God, who has saved us and called us to a holy life—not because of anything we have done but because of his own purpose and grace.

## 1 Pet. 1:3-5

Praise be to the God and Father of our Lord Jesus Christ! In his great mercy he has given us new birth into a living hope through the resurrection of Jesus Christ from the dead, and into an inheritance that can never perish, spoil or fade—kept in heaven for you, who through faith are shielded by God's power until the coming of the salvation that is ready to be revealed in the last time.

## 2 Pet. 1:3

His divine power has given us everything we need for life and godliness through our knowledge of him who called us by his own glory and goodness.

## Rev. 4:11

You are worthy, our Lord and God, to receive glory and honor and power, for you created all things, and by your will they were created and have their being.

## Rev. 19:1

After this I heard what sounded like the roar of a great multitude in heaven shouting: "Hallelujah! Salvation and glory and power belong to our God."

# NOTES

1. *Webster's New World Dictionary of the American Language*, 2d ed., s.v. "reconciliation."

2. Bill Hybels (in an interview with *Leadership Magazine*, "Standing in the Crossfire," Winter 1993, 14, 16).

3. Christian Community Church at Clarksville, Tennessee, http://www.christiancommunityclarksville.com/sermon_05-15-2005 .html (accessed October 2, 2006).

4. *Atlanta Journal-Constitution*, 30 June 2000.

5. MedicineNet.com, "MedTerms Dictionary," http://www.med terms.com/script/main/art.asp?articlekey=33842 (accessed October 2, 2006).

6. *Webster's New World Dictionary of the American Language*, 2d ed., s.v. "anger."

7. WordNet® 2.0, © 2003 Princeton University, http://wordnet .princeton.edu (accessed October 3, 2006).

8. *American Heritage Dictionaries*, s.v. "failure," http://www .answers.com/topic/failure (accessed October 2, 2006).

9. Thomas John Watson Sr., BrainyQuote.com, http://www .brainyquote.com/quotes/authors/t/thomas_john_watson_sr.html (accessed October 10, 2006).

10. Joyce Brothers, BrainyQuote.com, http://www.brainy quote.com/quotes/authors/j/joyce_brothers.html (accessed October 2, 2006).

11. Aristotle, BrainyQuote.com, http://www.brainyquote.com/ quotes/quotes/a/aristotle117887.html (accessed October 3, 2006).

# Are you discouraged

# with the way

# your life is going?

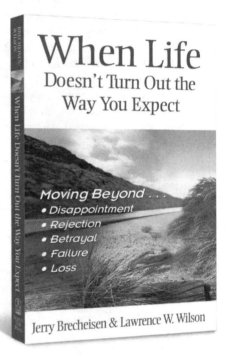

ISBN-13: 978-0-8341-2069-3

In *When Life Doesn't Turn Out the Way You Expect,* Jerry Brecheisen and Lawrence Wilson identify the negative effects of difficult life experiences and bring you to the point of healing the hurts and disappointments. You will relate to the stories of heartbreak, loss, rejection, and failure that parallel the authors' own difficult life experiences. Then they guide you to the point of healing—the place where God brings redemption to suffering.

# Look for it wherever Christian books are sold!

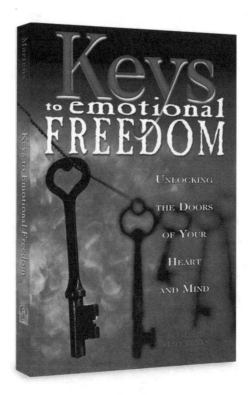